GOOD-BYE, MR. CHIPPENDALE

T. H. ROBSJOHN–GIBBINGS

Good-bye,
Mr. Chippendale

Illustrated by MARY PETTY

New York

ALFRED A. KNOPF

1 9 4 4

First and Second Printings before Publication
Third Printing, March 1944
Fourth Printing, April 1944
Fifth Printing, May 1944
Sixth Printing, August 1944

Published simultaneously in Canada by The Ryerson Press

Manufactured in the United States of America

TO

BILL B., AND FRED,
AND BECK

AUTHOR'S NOTE

The architecture and decoration mentioned in this book are real, and no reference is intended to anything imaginary.

ACKNOWLEDGMENTS

I wish to acknowledge my indebtedness to Mrs. Doris Campbell Bisonet, whose intelligent, devoted assistance and advice have been invaluable in the preparation of this book.

To attempt to list all the sources from which my material has been gathered would mean a listing of all the books on architecture and furniture which I have read over the past fifteen years. I would, however, like to acknowledge the kindness of Mr. William Helburn, who has given me access to his splendid architectural library, as well as guiding me to the sources of such information as I required. I wish also to thank Mr. Albert Duveen for information on the history of his family; and Mr. William Gilmore for many helpful suggestions.

I should like to record here the generosity of the following individuals and publishers who have given me permission to quote from their publications:

The American Mercury: Article in the June 1942 issue, "Thurman Arnold: Prophet of Prosperity" by William Bradford Huie.

Parke-Bernet Galleries: Sale catalogue of the Condé Nast Collection: "Condé Nast—A Recollection" by Elsie Mendl. "Condé Nast—As a Collector" by Frank Crowninshield.

Fortune: Article in the May 1931 issue, "Hearst at Home." Article in January 1942 issue, "Good-Bye Mr. Chippendale."

Harper's Bazaar: "Why Don't You" articles.

Pencil Points: Article in the December 1942 issue, "Yesterday, Today and Tomorrow" by Mary Heaton Vorse.

Retailing: Article in the March 15, 1943 issue, "OWI Praises New Plastic Navy Dishes."

The Studio Magazine: Article, "The Royal Academy Plan for Central London" by Professor C. H. Reilly.

Vogue: Condé Nast Publications, Inc., Copyright 1943.

DE WOLFE, ELSIE: *The House in Good Taste.* D. Appleton-Century Company; 1941, New York.

DRAPER, DOROTHY: *Decorating Is Fun.* Copyright, 1941, by Doubleday, Doran and Company, Inc., New York.

DUVEEN, JAMES HENRY: *Art Treasures and Intrigue.* Copyright, 1935, by Doubleday, Doran and Company, Inc., New York.

MORRISON, HUGH: *Louis Sullivan.* W. W. Norton & Company, Inc.; 1935, New York.

POST, EMILY: *The Personality of a House.* Funk & Wagnalls Company; 1930, New York.

SIRONEN, MARTA K.: *A History of American Furniture.* The Towse Publishing Co.; 1936, New York.

SULLIVAN, LOUIS: *Kindergarten Chats.* Permission through the courtesy of Mr. George G. Elmslie, literary executor of the Sullivan estate.

WHITMAN, WALT: *Leaves of Grass.* Copyright, 1924, by Doubleday, Doran and Company, Inc., New York.

WRIGHT, FRANK LLOYD: *Frank Lloyd Wright on Architecture.* Edited by Frederick Gutheim. Duell, Sloan & Pearce, Inc., 1941, New York.

T. H. ROBSJOHN-GIBBINGS

New York City, 1944

CONTENTS

I. LET'S FACE IT   3

II. ANTIQUE MORNING AFTER   7

III. WHO SAID WE ARE NOT AMUSED?   13

IV. TURNING THE TURKISH CORNER   21

V. ON THE AVENUE—FIFTH AVENUE   35

VI. LADIES' DAY   43

VII. MADAME, YOUR ANTIQUES ARE SHOWING   53

VIII. GOING—GOING— GONE   63

IX. BAUHAUS BLUES   71

X. CHARGE TO THE JURY   79

XI. THIS IS WHERE YOU CAME IN   83

XII. GO FORTH IN GOOD CHEER   103

SUGGESTED READING   109

1. LET'S FACE IT

"America, thou hast it better than our old Continent. Thou hast no ruined castles, no such geologic chaos. No useless memories of old history and futile strife vex thy inner spirit in this living hour. Use thy present time to the ends of good fortune! And when now thy children write, let them challenge with forthright skill knights, robbers, and ghost stories." GOETHE

THERE is a young generation of Americans to whom it seems as natural to find antique and reproduction furniture in the living room as it does to find an electric refrigerator in the kitchen. There are also Americans of an older generation who can remember the day when there was no such thing as antique furniture in America.

Few of these two generations even trouble their heads as to how this change in thinking came about, and no one to date has taken the trouble to tell them about it, much less point out the disastrous effect it has had on their lives.

One might almost say there is a conspiracy of censorship which protects the whole topic of antique furniture. Radio comedians might take a crack at it now and then for a laugh, but apart from this kind of familiarity, nobody seems to have nerve enough to break through the sentimentality and snobbery surrounding the antique world, and show the humbug and farce of its origin and perpetuation.

There are several reasons for this conspiracy of silence. Naturally the antique dealers aren't talking—it's their means of livelihood. It is also the livelihood of interior decorators, and the magazines that illustrate their efforts (and depend on their advertisements, which is much more to the point). But in addition to this, not even the writers of the more serious kind, who spend their lives on expensive books about antique furniture, ever tell the story of the *origin* of antique collecting.

[3]

It isn't a very pretty story, and if the American people really understood it, the whole carefully built-up structure of the antique legend would collapse. Neither dealers in antiques nor books about them would be needed. As far as I am concerned, the sooner the collapse comes the better; but that may be a one-man opinion. Meanwhile, I am going to tell the whole story. Let the chips fall where they may.

Humanity, we are told, is on the verge of new things. Mankind is stirring and on the march. And ahead is a post-war world filled with prospects for the realization of man's fondest and oldest dreams. Among them is a good home to live in.

This, at least, seems a reasonable and not unobtainable desire, and judging from architects' plans and the architectural magazines, much preparation for it is well in hand. But it seems to me that these architects, brilliant men though they obviously are, take for granted that the public is following step by step close behind them, ready for the post-war day when their housing plans materialize.

Something tells me that here the architects have lost touch with reality. The public is nowhere near them; in fact, when the day comes, these architects might well look around and find there isn't a soul in sight. The public will have dropped out miles behind to browse in an antique shoppe, refusing to go one more step of the way.

In general, the public does not read architectural magazines. They read the other kind (you know which I mean); and most of the contemporary thinking, as well as the contemporary architecture illustrated in the architectural magazines, could be going on in Mars as far as the average man or woman is concerned. They simply don't know about it, and they care even less.

Before anything can be done about all this, and certainly before any contemporary thinking about houses can become general, the antique legerdemain must be exposed for the disgraceful, anti-democratic, nonsensical, old-world hangover it really is —and this is the very moment to do it.

Building is at a standstill; furniture making in Grand Rapids is restricted (thank God); and we have a breathing spell to plan the kind of house we might have in a post-war world. It is vital that this consideration include a résumé of the origin and effect of antique furniture in America so that the post-war thinking may be that much clearer and that much more constructive.

In the thirty years between 1910 and 1940, according to official figures, approximately *one billion dollars* were spent in Europe buying antiques for American homes. Today hundreds of books are published tracing the history of antiques to encourage and inform the public and collectors. The reproduction of these antiques has been as high as ninety per cent of the total output of commercial furniture manufacturers. Schools, books, and magazines, teaching the theory of interior decoration in America, base their advice largely on the use of this antiques formula. The cumulative effect of this teaching has resulted in mass consciousness and mass acceptance of the whole idea.

Over one hundred years ago, Emerson said: "Our day of dependence, our long apprenticeship to the learning of other lands, draws to a close. The millions that around us are rushing into life, cannot always be fed on the sere remains of foreign harvests. Events, actions, arise, that must be sung, that will sing themselves."

But it is not true that the long apprenticeship has drawn to a close—nor is America completely free from the "sere remains of foreign harvests." These brave words are only a mockery as their challenge reaches us across the century. In the grim statistics on antiques which I have quoted, is the record of one remaining foreign harvest—and its colossal bill.

Now this is a more serious business than may at first appear, and just how serious it is was uncovered by the war emergency, when it suddenly became necessary to house millions of war workers.

The housing schemes that were to accomplish this vast undertaking were in contemporary design and were well advanced when it was discovered that there was no furniture in existence that would be really suitable for these new houses. The large overstuffed furniture and elaborately carved, ornate antique reproductions would look grotesque against the clean simplicity of the new interiors. There was practically *no contemporary American furniture to be found.* The entire commercial furniture industry had become rotten to the very core by decades of reproducing the antique furniture of Europe and Colonial America, a fact which few people realized until the needs of war brought the grim facts into the open.

I cannot believe that Americans will allow this to continue indefinitely. Surely the time has come at last when the paralyzing effect of this humbug must be broken. The nation that built the dams of the Tennessee River has not run out of ideas yet.

In the post-war years that lie ahead, America will be called upon to rehouse and provide furniture for millions of its people. We must prepare for this gigantic rehabilitation. So let's take a realistic look at the lumber rooms of Europe—think over the depressing saga that made us into antique collectors—and when we are through, examine our own good architecture and the possibilities for good contemporary American furniture.

2. ANTIQUE MORNING AFTER

"We might dwell at length upon the monstrous defects of a palace, so huge and so costly, with all its extravagant appendages. . . . Thus was wealth squandered upon what had been the haunt of snakes, frogs and toads. Such was the Kings' bad taste in all things." SAINT-SIMON

How did we get into this mood of bated breath about antiques? After all, it's one thing for senile octogenarians to polish up their old hickory pipe stands, but nowadays it seems that everyone is poking about in attics and olde quainte shoppes and bringing home some horror that in normal times would have ended its days quietly and decently in the scrap heap. I have seen hard-boiled Wall Street brokers and Broadway playwrights, week-ending in their pseudo-farmhouses in Bucks County, go right into a school-girl rave over a decrepit bedpan, with a look in their eyes that shouldn't have been there for anything less than the Holy Grail.

There must be an explanation for all this, so I began a little one-man investigation of the history books. At first plunge I got so helplessly balled up between *Das Möbel Werk*, Boffrand's *Livre D'Architecture*, three volumes on the Crystal Palace, and some old copies of *Vogue*, that I had dreams in which the Margravine, Valentina, and Prince Albert took over the decorating department at Lord & Taylor's. I soon snapped out of all that, and then, thank God, things settled down. I was able to take a cautious and realistic look at the eighteenth century, particularly the English part of it, and see what really went on around the bigshot cabinetmakers—Chippendale, Hepplewhite and Sheraton—the untouchable trinity of the antique legend.

I began with the boys and girls for whom this trio designed their furniture. There was, for instance, the whimsical Duchess of Portland, who "thought high birth preferable to all merit whatever." And Lady Pomfret, with a soothing comment on the Grand Tour: "Nothing can be more proper for a man of quality, capacity and fortune. Yet surely nothing can be more improper where these things are wanting." The Mesdames Portland and Pomfret, who were typical clients, were at least talkative.

The Grand Tour, by the way, was a trip through Europe, and particularly Italy, planned as a fitting climax to the education of the sons of rich eighteenth-century Englishmen. To further this, the Dilettanti Society was formed, a small and private club, which some abstemious archaeological killjoy hoped would dignify the looting of Greco-Roman objets d'art found en route. The real qualifications for membership, however, according to a crack Horace Walpole made, were "drunkenness and a visit to Italy," to which he adds that "the two chiefs of the Society, Lord Middlesex and Sir James Dashwood, were seldom sober the whole time they were there." Too bad the Pomfret girl could not have been on the dock when those two cards came pie-eyed off a windjammer, lugging a bust of Nero between them.

These English eighteenth-century millionaires, known to the innkeepers of Europe as "travelling English milords," grabbed up pictures and statuary by the coach-load, and hurried back with them to fill up the stately homes. A brisk business in this type of merchandise was carried on by the English consuls in Venice until the authorities clamped down and made an end to such unseemly shopkeeping.

There is a curious similarity between the doings of these travelling English millionaires and the equally travelling American millionaires who, unfortunately came more than one hundred and fifty years later, a similarity that should be kept well in mind in any review of the antiques racket as a whole. It is true, of course, that the English prototype did not go in for antique *furniture,* but the avidity with which he bought pictures by old masters and statuary by still older sculptors was exactly the same *nouveau riche* taste that Europeans thought so vulgar when indulged in by American millionaires in the nineteenth century.

Regarding the houses of the eighteenth-century English nobility, the general theory seemed to be fairly well summed up by one of their contemporaries who remarked that "being intended for elegance and magnificence, they must have the parts great." That this "elegance and magnificence" was varied according to the mere whims of these men and women, we also know from one of their favorite architects, Isaac Ware, who wrote (most indiscreetly): "We have seen architecture, a science founded upon the soundest principles, disgraced by ignorant caprice and fashion."

Finally, we have these rather solemn verdicts from two of the greatest authorities on the people of this period, Tipping and Stratton: "Their aesthetic spirit was one of choice exclusiveness and specialized artificiality. Grandeur reduced to rule was their aim. The word 'palatial' appealed to them excessively."

"These people did not need homes; they wanted halls and salons in which to display their carefully trained manners. They were indifferent to draughts, provided the rooms supplied the correct atmosphere of pomp and state. Their hearts were cold. They were dilettanti, amateurs in the true sense of the term, and their rooms corresponded to their social ideals."

So much then for the cabinetmakers' clients—those landowners and millionaire merchants, whose arrogant assumption that merit is synonymous with high birth, and whose alcoholic excesses and ignorant caprices had to be catered to.

Now for the cabinetmakers themselves, whose business it was to design and make and, above all, to *sell* furniture to this fashion-mad clientele. It was hard work for the boys, but they kept after it like overworked editors on *Harper's Bazaar*.

Chippendale, the Schiaparelli of the furniture creators, would bring out "Gothic" one season and "Chinese" the next. And he was quite willing to debase a design to the point of bankruptcy, if necessary, in order to catch the eye and anticipate the next folly. He admits quite frankly in his own book of designs that his aim was to provide furniture "in the most fashionable taste."

Hepplewhite was also realistic about the whole set-up, and says in his *Repository of Designs* that he "designedly followed the latest or most prevailing fashion only."

One cabinetmaker, lashed into a frenzy by this fashionable scene-shifting, advertised in 1757: "All sorts of Rooms after the manner of the Arabian, Chinese, Persian, Gothic, Muscovite, Palladian, Roman, Vitruvian, and Egyptian." Coney Island itself couldn't offer more.

But it is Sheraton who is really quite brutal about the whole thing, going out of his way, to crab the hell out of his predecessors —Hepplewhite, Chippendale, and everybody else he could think of. Chippendale, he says, "is wholly antiquated and laid aside," and then goes on to tackle Hepplewhite, saying: "Compared with the newest taste, his work has already caught the decline, and, perhaps in a little time will suddenly die in the disorder."

Then he sums up what he considers the entire folly of the eighteenth-century cabinetmakers as shown in their books of design, saying sadly of them; ". . . through change of fashions they are become obsolete." That comes from Sheraton himself, a hundred and fifty years ago.

The shrewd eyes of Horace Walpole (perhaps the most discerning of his day) saw through this flossy fandango, and he made no bones about saying so. The Gothic and Chinese styles, so exciting to Chippendale, he called "Bastard Gothic" and "Mongrel Chinese," while the work of Adam, the extra-elegant architect, was like "gingerbread and snippets of embroidery . . . filligrane and fan painting." And the canopied bed Adam concocted for Osterley looked to him "like a modern headdress . . . decorated by a milliner."

Far be it from me to be iconoclastic, but what appeared to be millinery in 1778 you must agree might now be described as quite definitely "old hat," or as Sheraton gloomily predicted, "obsolete."

You may ask, not unreasonably, just what is all this historical muck raking leading up to?

Well, this is the point I am trying to make: The well-known cabinetmakers, who have been glorified as "old masters" by the writers of eulogistic furniture tomes, by the dealers, and by the auctioneers, were often rather grandiose and ridiculous themselves. Far from being interested in good design, actually they were desperately anxious to indulge the nobility and whip together novel forms of grandomania for pompous houses. They were completely at one with the accepted orgy of palatial ostentation that the European aristocracy of the eighteenth century wallowed in. This passion for the gigantic and elaborately fashionable, amounting to megalomania, goaded on the architects and furniture designers, until it looked, as one observer of the time said, as if "all the world was mad on building as far as they could reach." To which one might add that in the miles of gilded stucco, and in the tortured furniture crowding the salons of eighteenth-century Europe, this particular madness achieved an all-time high in over-reaching.

Today, by some sort of ridiculous mental jugglery, we attempt to disassociate this furniture from the conditions which produced it. It would seem to me that a chair which was deliberately over-designed to express the fashionable ostentatious mentality of its owner two hundred years ago is still an over-designed and ostentatious chair today.

Our acceptance of the "perfect taste" of past European *folie de grandeur* is due for what actors call a "double take," and the sooner we get around to this second look, the clearer our true assessment of it will be. The whole delusion becomes increasingly absurd, when we study the origins of antique furniture collecting. But that quaint saga of Victorian gullibility has a chapter all to itself.

As Napoleon said when he quit: "Cette vielle Europe m'ennuie," It bores me too, so let's get out of here!

3. WHO SAID WE ARE NOT AMUSED?

"In England, for example, our basins, ewers, jugs, and all vessels for washing are of countless varieties of form and of colossal proportions compared to those of any other country. Future ages will infer from the crockery of our bedrooms that we were giants in these our days, and will lament over their own degeneracy. On the other hand a moderate sized milk jug or tart pan satisfy all the ablutionary wants of a Frenchman or woman."

WANDERINGS IN THE CRYSTAL PALACE
THE ART JOURNAL — 1851

THE eighteenth-century architectural burlesque was over. The curtain line—the Royal Pavilion at Brighton—was a belly laugh. Grotesque and preposterous, it was, according to Hazlitt, the result of "the genius of architecture having the dropsy and megrims." The offspring of this monster, reaching full maturity sixty-four years later, was the Crystal Palace. By then the eighteenth century and its splurging celebrities had become the homespun, down-to-earth Victorians; and cast iron, not royalty, had become their god.

At this point we don't need to go into a long dissertation on how the Victorians succeeded in wiping out so completely the architecture and furniture of the preceding period, and how they replaced it with the alternative horror forever designated by the name of the Queen. It all had something to do with the blue bloods not being quite so fashionable. Their cynicism had become *démodé*, their arrogance a bore. The French Revolution was the end of their long-term contract, and the gangsters of the Industrial Revolution were taking over the rule of the world. (The new *middle* classes were on their own, and, being no longer dependent on the cast-off styles of a ruling aristocracy, they dreamed up an appalling specialty for themselves. This, however, is by the way. It is really the gangsters of big business that we have to keep our minds on, because they are the clue to the antique-furniture mystery.)

These were the boys who overnight became as rich as the gentry; and the hair-raising story of their exploitation of men, women, and children in their factories makes one realize that the outward respectability and sentimentality of the Victorians concealed the same vicious social cruelty of the previous century.

The results of sweated labor were refreshing profits for the owners. These profits meant power, and that meant a brisk business over the peerage counter. Soon the House of Lords was echoing to the Lancashire and Yorkshire accents of cotton spinners, soap plutocrats, tobacco tycoons and bejewelled brokers who were "in t'brass." The older aristocracy, unable to attack the power of these upstart *nouveaux riches,* succeeded in sneering them into the old sense of class inferiority. And so these industrial bullies, at this point in their expensive climb, became cringing and anxious to be indistinguishable from the haughty survivors of older titles.

There was nothing particularly baffling about these blue-blooded survivors. The key to an understanding of them was the perpetual repetition of their way of living, the emptiness of which was constantly overlooked as the repetitions multiplied and became tradition.

Immutably fixed, withdrawn into their vast acreage, the houses of the old rich were the same opulent hulks of previous centuries—a little shabbier now, with the original swagger gone out of them, but still possessing the furniture Chippendale and his contemporaries had made. The gilt was peeling from the carved mirror frames, the mahogany had lost its freshness, but since change was abhorrent they remained fixed in time.

The middle classes were on their own

Of all this the industrial millionaires gradually became aware. This they saw was the real McCoy! But what to do? How could they become "landed gentry" overnight, when it had taken some of the squirarchy hundreds of years to get that way?

Obviously something had to be done to achieve a metamorphosis in a fraction of this time. How simple it would be, for instance, if one could buy the stately bit, lock, stock and barrel, and just move right in. A few coats of arms would have to be changed, of course, but that would be all.

Some of the old estates were for sale: "Nobleman's private landed estate, 70,000 acres (sporting and pastoral), including picturesque Georgian residence. Finely timbered park with lodge at entrance. Spring-fed lake well stocked with coarse fish. Also three grouse moors."

How much?

Here was the way to wipe out the stains of the sweatshops. Who would know that their *own* ancestors had not lived there one hundred, two hundred, three, four, five hundred years ago?

Finally the new millionaires got "settled in"—not all of them in old houses, of course, because the supply was limited (though many of the "upper classes" sold out for a packet, as you can well imagine). Some of them had to build their own "baronial halls," usually "as perfect as could be wished in the style of mediaeval Gothic, with a fancy taste, and simple grandeur of contour."

But furniture, similar to that of the aristocracy, was needed. This was more difficult to supply, because at the time these industrial millionaires went on their ancestor-shopping spree, there was no such thing as a "dealer in antique furniture." There did exist, of course, the curiosity shops described by Dickens. There were also a few second-hand furniture dealers, but never

in their wildest dreams had they labelled their shabby wares
"antiques." Very few people knew the difference between the
styles of the early cabinetmakers. They were much too interested
in the confections of the period, definitely preferring papier-
mâché à la Victoria to Chippendale à la Française, even if they
could have recognized the latter as such.

Obviously someone was badly needed to get inside the old
houses and snaffle some of their contents. Soon enough, men
appeared for the job. In the beginning these men were simply
furniture dealers, but as they became aware of the great demand
for the old furniture, they naturally decided to supply it—as
"antique dealers."

These new antique dealers developed as a result of the snobbish demands of the new millionaires. The type of furniture
wanted was not on the market. It could be found only in the
houses of the older aristocracy, and it never occurred to the
owners to sell any of their possessions. But the opportunity to
get the furniture came when additions were made to the old
mansions. A new wing might be added to one of the stately
homes. Usually the architecture of the original was totally dis-
regarded because, ironically, even the older families preferred
the Victorian in architecture and furniture. The dealer would
supply them with brand-new furniture (brass beds, horsehair upholstery, Turkey carpets, etc.), and would make an agreement
that in payment he would take so much cash and some pieces of
old furniture from the original house—usually damaged pieces
that had been put in the housekeeper's room, the lodge, or sometimes even in the stables.

In time, of course, the owners of the old houses caught on,
but by then it was too late. Their antique loot had been spirited
away, and the furniture dealer was through forever with new

brass beds and new horsehair furniture. He now specialized only in antiques and fancy profits.

In the history of the Duveen family, perhaps the greatest name in antique and picture dealing, we have a typical example of the obscure origin of the antique dealer.

The great-grandparents of the present generation, fleeing Jewish persecution, settled in the eighteenth century in Meppel, Holland. Their son was a salesman in lard, travelling to Hull in England. Here he met Rosetta Barnett, daughter of a pawn-broker. As a token of his regard for her, he used to bring her an occasional piece of Dutch Delft pottery, never realizing, of course, its value to early collectors in England.

One day it dawned on Rosetta's father that there was a market for such wares, and Duveen and he went into business selling porcelains. In their trips to London, the pair saw the first of the new millionaires prowling around looking for other old things besides porcelain and pottery.

Duveen married Rosetta, and Joseph (later Lord Duveen of Milbank) was their first-born. The business in porcelains grew, and the family moved to Oxford Street in London. By this time they decided to include some old furniture among their wares, and soon became "antique dealers."

The industrious and God-fearing years marched on. Then on January 22, 1901, Queen Victoria died, and the twentieth century, like an impatient heir who has suffered too long under the tyranny of an old-fashioned benefactor, took over the fun that had started with the champagne nineties. The Widow of Windsor was gone. Society and Royalty came back with a bang. No play was complete without a duchess or two. And novelists concocted a mirage of high life in which dukes cluttered the pages more than murderers do now.

The middle classes lived in an imaginary orgy of getting into society—needless to add, without ever getting there. They now took the same avid interest in the "landed gentry" that the industrial millionaires had taken originally, with the result that they also decided antique furniture was "very natty," and "the thing."

The collectomania started with pewter plates, samplers, toby jugs, and Tudor oak, and went on from there into everything the afflicted could lay their hands on. The dealers were in clover. But there were not enough "goods" for the growing demand, though they scoured the country, insinuating their way into remote cottages and vicarages in a feverish search for it. Still there was not enough, and something had to be done. It was.

Since the days of the Graeculi Delirantes, as the Romans called them (crazy Greeks to you), who probably started the whole thing, experts at faking have always existed. They soon tumbled to the idea of what the new antique-furniture dealers needed, and got busy.

Hidden deep in the alleys of Tottenham Court Road, they took the unsaleable Elizabethan beds, converted the backs into overmantels, and used the posts as legs of the then much valued bulbous-legged refectory tables. They cut down tripod mahogany banner screens, and fitted a top to make Chippendale tables. They employed dozens of girls to weave copies of old designs in needle-work, which were then stained with coffee and left in the rain for a week or two. Old walnut doors became "Queen Anne corner-cupboards." Old mahogany chests had their faces lifted, and made their second debut as priceless "Chippendale." Miles of old and not-so-old pine floorboards appeared as eighteenth-century rooms "taken from a house at Norwich." In Florence and Venice "old" candelabra, andirons, gates, lamps, and everything the tourist was looking for were manufactured by the thousands.

In Belgium, there flourished factories to turn out the arms and armor without which no early period room was complete. In Cologne, "Roman" glass was produced by the ingenious method of leaving it in manure for a few weeks.

One expert said twenty years ago of the Paris antique business: "In principle there is no such thing as antique furniture. All that is sold is false or terribly repaired." And ten years later, Herbert Cescinsky, the outstanding authority on antique furniture, states: "There are thousands of really clever men engaged in forging objects which are high priced enough to make the game worth while. Yet we expect the dealer to know more than the whole army of these fakers put together."

While all this shenanigan was getting under way, the Edwardian proletariat, hungry for information on the newly intriguing dukes and duchessess and their past history in the stately homes, started out on an unprecedented sight-seeing tour. Derelict palaces, ruined castles, and "birthplaces" were hastily dusted off, and prices of admission decided on. Four-horse wagonettes and "tourist trains" carried the new audience to the remote corners of Europe to gape at the seedy grandeur of the past. Owners of "famous" houses, who for generations had had no occasion to admit commoners except as servants were now so flattered by this popular adulation that they set aside a day in the week during which the house was "on view."

On this day of condescension, awe-stricken whispering groups, led by a footman, trailed bug-eyed from the banqueting hall to "the bedroom Queen Elizabeth slept in." As they proceeded, they listened to the fascinating and always daring exploits of the eighth and tenth h'earl, the only pauses in the exalted historiette being when they were cautioned, "Don't touch please."

The next step in this mass canonization of the obsolete was

inevitable. Everything possible must be "put in a museum," or made a "national monument," to which it was expected that generations of the pious would make their pilgrimages. Funds were raised by governments, town councils, and individuals, and soon throughout Europe no town, however small, was without some dingy building, set apart to house a conglomeration of dusty objects, usually ranging from mouldy travel memorabilia contributed by the local nobility to Roman fragments dug up by the local farmer.

People who for generations had taken it for granted that you bought new furniture when you built a house, now thought only in terms of antiques.

The tocsin had sounded for the furniture designers of the world. The continuity of their long history reaching back to remote time was broken. The furniture of their dead predecessors was rising like a flood, and they could copy or forge this furniture —or starve.

Only one thing more was needed now to foment the fanaticism to the ultimate limits of the preposterous, and the moment was at hand. The millionaires of America were landing at Southampton and Cherbourg.

"Don't touch, please!"

4. TURNING THE TURKISH CORNER

"Insist on yourself; never imitate. Your own gift you can present every moment with the cumulative force of a whole life's cultivation; but of the adopted talent of another you have only an extemporaneous half possession."

EMERSON

On August 19, 1854, the *New York Times* published a brief obituary: "In this city on Wednesday August 16, Duncan Phyfe died in the eighty-sixth year of his life." In these few words, finis was written to the last disciple in the United States who had carried over the traditions of the English eighteenth-century cabinetmakers—particularly those of Sheraton. With his death, America was finally on her own.

In the new world, free from the European tradition of over-elaboration, there were soon definite signs of a development of a new style of furniture. In 1865, a Mr. John K. Mayo of New York City took out a patent for plywood. In the next fifteen years, designers everywhere were boldly experimenting with ideas in furniture that were as new as the skyscrapers that followed them.

A bent plywood chair was designed in 1874 that makes today's Aalto chair look like a reincarnation. Five years later, a designer in New York conjured out of thin air an adjustable reclining chair of metal, which beat Le Corbusier to it by half a century. Another bright soul invented a compact bedroom unit including a double bed, shoedrawers, shelving to store clothes, and a washstand—a forerunner of all today's space-saving devices. Passengers on ferryboats and railroad trains were sitting on curved and perforated plywood seats, the first of their kind in the world, and a forgotten forerunner of the contemporary plywood furniture being manufactured by much-touted European designers today. Yet another innovation in furniture design originated in America: the idea of sectional furniture, which is now one of the basic principles of contemporary furniture design.

I particularly mention this flurry of new world activity because we should be quite clear in our minds that some of the principles of contemporary furniture had already appeared here before the snobbism over European furniture swamped the American mentality.

One of the more celebrated pioneers of a long line of his type who helped to create the snobbism and the misbegotten aesthetic taste of the new world was Sir Charles Eastlake, an English architect, whose book, *Hints on Household Taste,* reached America in 1867.

"Eastlakeism" was a godawful Gothic hash. It turned American houses into the nightmare backgrounds reproduced so effectively in the movie, *The Magnificent Ambersons.* Though its vogue was short, it put ideas into the heads of the furniture manufacturers and the public, who followed it up with an equally messy variation on the style of Queen Anne, to say nothing of a little Orientalia.

The latter was brought on perhaps unknowingly by another titled gent, Sir Richard Burton, with his unexpurgated edition of the *Arabian Nights.* This salacious titbit, working like an aphrodisiac on the home furnishers of America, excited them to moments of downright abandon, if not complete nymphomania. Pictures of steaming harems by Gérôme hung cheek-by-jowl with statuettes of dancing girls, whose bronze skirts, hinged to open and show the nudity inside (remember?), led on to the final concentrated mash of the Turkish corner, which erupted hubble-bubble pipes, tiger skins, oriental rugs, mosque lamps and voluptuous divans.

In all this imported decorative pandemonium, no one in America had yet suggested that actual antique furniture should be bought, but in view of what was happening to the industrial magnates of Europe, this cajolery was only a matter of time.

Looking a little like Julian Eltinge doing a *male* impersonation, Oscar Wilde sashayed into America in January 1882, and after looking around said of American cities: "There is a good deal of beauty to be seen in them now and then, but only where the American has not attempted to create it." The houses, he said, were "illy designed, decorated shabbily, and in bad taste." "Be early English," he pleaded with stars in his eyes, "before it is too late." Coming from a pre-Raphaelite dude in satin pants, this message was big stuff. The antique itch was under way. And ten years later, the rush began when the gates opened on the Chicago World's Fair.

This carousal of European taste was like the shot of a starting pistol for architects, antique dealers, and the public in a race to revive what they thought were the great classic traditions of the past.

Louis Sullivan, the lonely pioneer of a contemporary American architecture, looked with horror at the Fair's be-domed "palaces" filled with borrowed European art and said with prophetic bitterness: "The damage wrought to this country by the Chicago World's Fair will last half a century." The half century is up. Mr. Sullivan had underestimated the time and the damage.

The effect of the Fair can be judged by an advertisement in 1894 of the Popular Shop, owned by Joseph P. McHugh and Company, on West Forty-second Street and Fifth Avenue: "A room in the old Dutch fashion is hung with a Delft blue paper," runs this advertisement, "Beyond, a lofty room is filled with high-backed easy chairs in the old English style, the walls hung with antique tapestries of Flemish origin.

"A room of golden tone has furniture and hangings suggestive of the Louis XIV period.

"Another hung in scarlet canvas shows carved grilles and seats in the Florentine style, and there is a dainty Colonial room in cool mignonette green."

Mr. McHugh's shop was typical of the period. It combined decorating, antique dealing, and Liberty silks in one solid lump. However, in 1895 when "Americans began to spend their summers in wandering through old palaces and castles 'on the other side'" (as *Vogue* described it), women decorators and antique dealers began to appear as separate units. The first woman decorator to become famous was, of course, Elsie de Wolfe.

Miss de Wolfe, after a childhood in a brownstone house on the site now occupied by Macy's department store, was presented to Queen Victoria in the eighties, was the first professional actress to be invited to the Bachelors' Cotillion in the nineties, and became an interior decorator at the turn of the century. Time marches on.

The fleeting brush with royalty, the palaces, the duchesses, the castles, and particularly the period furniture of France inspired her first and last love, and in 1904, when she opened shop, they were the stuff that the dreams of her clients were also made on. Nothing, it seemed to her and to them, could be more appropriate than to house the industrial kings of America in the antiquated surroundings of the Bourbons. And this Elsie de Wolfe did superbly.

She had appeared at the precise moment when the snobbish passion for European manners and décor was beginning to devour the women of America, and her influence in cultivating this disas-

trous fashion was responsible for its spreading far beyond the
millionaires who came into personal contact with her.

Of all that remains of the early years of the century, there is
no more fascinating document of Americana than a book called
The House in Good Taste, published in 1913, in which Miss
de Wolfe sets forth the secrets of her craft. Decoratively speaking, American women live in the shadow of Elsie de Wolfe, and
if it was the Chicago World's Fair that kept American architecture back fifty years, it was she who did the same thing for
American furniture design.

Should this suggestion make you writhe in your bergère chair,
or wince under the *couvre-pieds* of your chaise longue, or pale
against your *boiserie*, I hasten to spread out on the Aubusson rug
some blossoms garnered from the parterres of Miss de Wolfe's
garden of décor.

"Men are forever guests in our homes," says the authoress on
page 5, "no matter how much happiness they may find there."
Vaguely haunted by this edict, I read on until on page 169, I
came face to face with the usurpers of American manhood: "I
love to house my little people happily—my dogs and my birds and
my fish. Wee Toi, my little Chinese dog, has a little house all
his own, an old Chinese lacquer box with a canopy top and little
gold bells. . . . The aquarium . . . delights my soul . . . it
is the home of the most gorgeous fan-tailed goldfish. I was so
pleased with the aquarium and the lacquer bed for Wee Toi, I
devised a birdcage . . . of gilt wires . . . the nicest place you
can imagine for a whistling bullfinch to live in. I suppose I could
have a Persian cat and a gorgeous cushion to complete the place,
but I can't admit cats into the room. I plan gorgeous cushions
for *other* people's 'little people' when they happen to be cats."

For a generation of homeless American males and their sons,

tinkering in their garages, or hiding in the attic, it might be
well to ponder on the ghosts of Wee Toi, gorgeous fantailed goldfish, whistling bullfinches, and possibly Persian cats.

It was Elsie de Wolfe's incredible contention that a Louis XVI
house was the ultimate limit in design, and that given heating
and sanitation it was the best that could be done in the way of a
modern house, now and forever.

She writes that at the time of Louis XVI, "the idea of the
modern house came into its own, and it could advance—as an
idea—hardly any further.

"For with all the intrepidity and passion of the later eighteenth
century in its search for beauty, for all the magic-making of con-
venience and ingenuity of the nineteenth century, the funda-
mentals have changed but little. And now we of the twentieth
century can only add material comforts and an expression of our
personality. . . .

"And so we women have achieved a house, luminous with kind
purpose throughout. It is finished—that is our difficulty! We
inherit it, all rounded in its perfection, consummate in its charms,
but it is finished, and what can we do about a thing that is
finished?"

Having proved conclusively (!) the hopelessness of any rash
attempts that Americans might make to design a more appropriate architecture for themselves, the author also warns them
not to be equally foolish with regard to furniture:

"We have not succeeded in creating a style adapted to our
modern life. It is just as well! Our life, with its haste, its nervous-
ness, and its preoccupations, does not inspire the furniture-
makers. We cannot do better than to accept the standards of
other times, and adapt them to our uses."

To attest these misbegotten convictions, *The House in Good*

The Turkish Corner

Taste ends with a description of the finding and purchase and restoration of the Villa Trianon, with a private entrance through the vegetable garden into the park of Versailles itself. The Villa was shared by Miss Elizabeth Marbury, and when the ladies were finally installed, they felt they "were living in a modern version of the Sleeping Beauty, with the sleeping villa for heroine."

Lulled by this olde worlde somnambulism, and the social aura artfully wreathed about it, hundreds of rich American women dreamed of doing likewise, or else becoming interior decorators and setting up shop for themselves.

Their poorer sisters, wide awake commercially at least, hopped down for a job at *Au Quatrième*, the antique section of Wanamaker's New York department store, where many a girl who is successful on Fifty-seventh Street today, started her long career in antiquity. *Au Quatrième*, opened in 1914, was inspired by the success of Elsie de Wolfe, and did a rip-snorting business. Incidentally, it was the origin of the "corner shoppes" which appeared later in most department stores throughout America.

While the inmates of this genteel seraglio at Wanamaker's hurried back and forth to loot "la belle France," other forces were appearing, eager for their share of the antique bazaar. These new arrivals were the antique dealers of Europe. Fresh and rich from their early triumphs with the Victorian millionaires at home, they saw that one more killing could be made in America, and rushed a large part of their stocks over the Atlantic.

We have a fascinating glimpse of the attitude of many of these dealers towards America and Americans, particularly those latter who were in the market for antiques. James Henry Duveen, in his book *Art Treasures and Intrigue*, writing of P. A. B. Widener of Philadelphia, frankly states:

"Like most of his contemporaries, Widener began to collect

in the early days, when collecting in America was the joke of the Old World. All the European fakers worked with an eye on the rich American, a sport which has not quite died out even yet. The more fantastically untrue a story connected with a picture or work of art, the more likely was it to find an eager buyer among the flocks of rich Americans who vied with each other in buying the bed Queen Elizabeth (or Empress Josephine, or Cleopatra—or all three!) had slept in."

If Elsie de Wolfe saw American houses as a divertissement in which Wee Toi *chinoiserie,* Trianon Villas, and whistling bullfinches played a part, these European dealers had other notions equally waggish.

The British contingent had two ideas—Early British and Late British. Any other form of antiquity and all women dealing in it were regarded as unimportant. While Elsie's siren song *à la Française* lured the *women* of America, the more sonorous voices of the British protagonists bade their menfolk to stuff their ears and hold on to more solid things.

Charles Duveen, whose activities went under the title of "Charles of London" was the big shot of these *exaltés* of bulldog antiquity. "Mr. Charles" saw art from an Elizabethan viewpoint, and expected others to share unconditionally the angle of his vision. "You can't beat it" was his succinct argument and the summing up of his implicit faith. This Tudoresque beef-à-la-mode came from a special recipe of imported ingredients, in which Mr. Charles had practically cornered the market.

We accept today as a kittenish fantasy of Longchamp's advertising department the idea of having "a glorious time with a pretty papoose" in their new Pow Wow room, but fifteen-odd years ago Charles of London evidently saw his clients in all seriousness as roguish doxies of Merrie England. Otherwise there can be no possible reason for the conversion of an apartment in the Hotel Plaza into an Elizabethan long-gallery, or the reproduction of Hampton Court in Westchester.

If Charles of London had appropriated the dismantled rooms and disused furnishings of the Tudors for his merchandise, his co-patriot, Sir Charles Allom, had bought up the preceding Gothic antiquities as his specialty. Sir Charles, from his London emporium in Hanover Square, had tinkered with the dukeries for years before he decided to peddle his wares on Madison Avenue. His lordship's conception of the grand chic was an enormous room with a carved timbered ceiling, a massive hooded stone fireplace, a refectory table, and—when the going was good —a Gothic tapestry. And believe me, in these early days the going in such tapestries was plenty good.

Sir Charles could be persuaded to run up a little Georgian décor now and again, the sort that as a board room in England brings grunts of approval, but it always seemed he was hesitant of this period. And rightly so. It was English Gothic that was his pièce de résistance.

While the Messrs. Duveen and Allom went about their little businesses, the Duveen first-born, Sir Joseph, also kept shop at the corner of Fifth Avenue and Fifty-sixth Street. Joe was now a millionaire merchant of the old masters, and as such is hardly within the scope of this modest homily on antique furniture. However, he must not be entirely omitted, because, in character with his penchant for the super-de-luxe, his stock included some tapestries and some French furniture. This furniture—not the kind you mark down for stock-taking—was labelled "grand palais," in stark contrast to that of competitors like Elsie de Wolfe, whose chefs-d'œuvre were merely "petit palais."

To complete the quintet of dogged pioneers came French and

Company, which originated in America, as far as I am aware. At a cursory glance, one might think the first four had the market covered, but there was splendid picking left in the vogue for the Italian, Spanish, and French Renaissance, and French and Company got this meaty morsel practically to themselves.

It was Fenway Court, a Venetian palace built in Boston in 1903, together with the gondolas and lagoons at the Chicago Fair ten years earlier, that sent Americans on the Italian hayride, which ended in such a shambles at Palm Beach, Miami Beach, and Alice Foote MacDougall's Coffee Shops. Of course, in the early years of the century, this gaudy finale was undreamed of. Italian seemed classic, and also "classy." *St. Ursula's Dream*, a painting by Carpaccio, inspired hundreds of bedrooms similar to the one in which the Saint is taking a nap; and the Davanzati Palace in Florence was as familiar to the Italian-minded as Whistler's mother was to their parents.

Those were the days, so help me, when it was the height of something to sit on a *cassapanca* upon a tiled floor, amid frescoed walls and coffered ceiling—an interior of incredible gloom, into which the daylight struggled (to the point of exhaustion) through picturesque leaded windows.

French and Company varied their Renaissance repertoire with a spectacular charade called French Gothic, in which saints appeared in stone niches, fires crackled in caverns of carved stone, candles flickered from wrought iron torchères, and finger bowls seemed to contain nothing less than holy water.

This confusion of the ecclesiastical and the secular, the result of too many visits to European churches and cathedrals by the American laity, struck few if any as incongruous. It seemed natural to hang your pants over a prie-dieu, keep the telephone book on a lectern, the cigars in a gutted hymnal, drape the walls with chasubles, put a chalice on the piano, and stand dolorous carved saints in the odd corners. Wall Street brokers revelled in this particular form of decorative bathos; and its probable palliative effect on their more private moments must be something for the reminiscences of many an aging Ziegfeld girl today.

Following the leading characters in the antique circus came a host of smaller fry, who specialized in the seventeenth-century walnut of Queen Anne and the eighteenth-century mahogany of Chippendale, Hepplewhite and Sheraton; but the taste for their particular wares came a little later than for those of the big five antique dealers.

In a most extraordinary way, the aesthetic taste of American millionaires from about 1900 to 1930 is typified in William Randolph Hearst. Any week-end visitor today at San Simeon, his summer palace in California, steps back into the days when men like Hearst gorged themselves on the salesrooms of Europe and New York, where their passion for the grandiose and the over-elaborate could be fed to repletion.

Here, according to *Fortune*, May 1931, is a description of his hideaway:

"In the fabulous Casa Grande . . . and in the great guest houses surrounding that enormous building, are chefs-d'œuvre from the collection of the greatest collector of objets d'art in the world. They fill the acres of great halls, guest rooms, bowling alleys, refectories, libraries, movie theatres, swimming pools, and elevators; they overflow the vast two-acre cellar which underlies La Casa Grande; they are dammed into a mountain of packing cases a block long which lies, weathering in the sun, at the foot of the hill. And, closer to their sources, they are dammed into a block-square storage house at 143rd Street off Southern Boulevard in New York City, which must now acquire more acres to hold them, even great San Simeon being inadequate. . . .

"The great storehouse off Southern Boulevard . . . In effect, it holds the bag for Mr. Hearst to pop treasures into. A nod at an auction, and anything from a snuffbox to a Spanish castle may turn up. . . . Broadly speaking this reservoir feeds four principal Hearst art repositories. One: the house at Riverside Drive . . . Two: St. Donat's Castle in Wales . . . Three: the recently purchased Belmont estate at Sands Point, Long Island . . . Four: San Simeon. . . . The Sands Point estate, which Mrs. Belmont called Beacon Towers, Mr. Hearst renamed St. Joan. This is a French chateau. . . . To Saint Donat's Castle often go objets d'art which have already crossed the ocean once to the central distributing point."

From this gigantic magpie's nest of antiquity, Mr. Hearst has selected for his dining room at San Simeon a Gothic stone chimney piece, Italian refectory tables, Flemish tapestries, seventeenth-century Spanish candlesticks, and some Georgian silver for the sideboard. One hundred and fifty people can drop in and take "pot luck," since it is solemnly affirmed that this is a ranch in which the spirit is that of camping out.

This familiarity with the over-bedizened was reflected in Hollywood, the next door neighbor of La Casa Grande. In those early days there was a striking similarity in the gaudy doings of Theda Bara and the décor to the north of her.

We see in the perspective of time that Mr. Hearst's taste was typical of all his contemporaries, and more important still, it was typical of the antique dealers' tastes at that time. The American and European antique dealers, together with their clients, had lived their childhood in a hangover of the Victorian varnished-oak Gothic revival. This elaborate, carved mediaeval style was reserved for dining-rooms, libraries, and some bedroom suites.

The style of the parlors was called "Frenchy." It was a travesty of Louis XV and XVI, with spindly gilt furniture upholstered in velvet and trimmed with ball fringe.

These caricatures of European styles were ridiculous in America, and the people who grew up in such rooms were taught by the antique dealers to scoff at these early excesses of the gilded age. Ironically enough, however, the Gothic of Sir Charles Allom, the Elizabethan of Charles of London, and the Renaissance of French and Company, did nothing toward altering this earlier taste. They merely replaced its sham antiquity with the genuine article. For instance, in the dining rooms and libraries, they replaced the varnished yellow oak with antique oak panelling; they replaced the William Morris tapestry wallpapers with Flemish and Gothic tapestries; the carved sham-mediaeval pier tables with Elizabethan court-cupboards or Gothic armoires; the carpets with Persian rugs; and the nineteenth-century velvet portieres with seventeenth-century portieres. In the parlors, the decorators replaced the spindly, gilt parlor suite with antique gilt bergère chairs and sofas, and the elaborate "Frenchy" draperies with the authentic toile de Jouy. In other words, they carried the Victorian misconception of a French parlor to the ultimate limits of an authentic eighteenth-century French salon. The dealers who shipped over the Queen Anne and eighteenth-century mahogany replaced, of course, the bastard versions of both those specialties.

At this point, having plucked and roasted the major fry of the antique world, we might digress for a moment and brood over the accessory question, and particularly the early flowering of the art of lamp-making. Hitherto lamps had been rather mundane things, but now they achieved "artistic" heights—and prices undreamed of before the days of antique collecting.

When the last bergère chairs or Elizabethan court-cupboards were in place, came the moment for the lamps. You, being a dead pigeon, might use a hunk of priceless rose quartz for a base, with a fringed shade of painted chiffon; or a *famille noir* vase with a fringed dome of antique taffeta. Both would be equally chic, and either would set you back anything up to fifteen grand. But believe me, the effect was a knockout. For the boudoir, came lamp numeros in bisque and Chelsea porcelain. Both were eighteenth-century groups of figures artfully sylvan, usually symbolizing Marie Antoinette as a milkmaid, dallying beside a shame-faced, beflowered cow. In Chelsea, the effect is similar to technicolor; in bisque, the figures appear as bloodless as a poltergeist. You took your choice.

Telephones at this time were quite a problem, and were considered a jarring note, obviously out of keeping in the olde worlde atmosphere. One method of overcoming this was that adopted by a lady in Paris who sent her messages by a live blackamoor. This was tempting, but New York was no place for such goings-on. Most period lovers concealed the awkward instrument under even more awkward china dolls with hoop skirts, while the extremists put a gilded sedan chair in the hall, and hopped in and out for a call to the drugstore or a chat.

A gilded sedan chair for a call to the drugstore

5. ON THE AVENUE—FIFTH AVENUE

AMERICA—*"It is the land of desire for all those who are weary of the historical lumber-room of old Europe."*   H E G E L

"WHEN good Americans die they go to Paris," was Oscar Wilde's overworked aphorism of the nineteenth century. But until that paradisiacal bliss could be finally attained, rich Americans prepared themselves by importing Parisian ideas in architecture.

There were many of these ideas, all of them bad, all of them copies of previous periods, or a mélange of several, but all tempting to the American plutocracy. What the American *nouveaux riches* and the travelling women decorators and architects found when they arrived in Europe was a bad copy of something that was cursed with over-elaboration even in its original form. The Industrial Revolution had filled Europe with a new class of millionaires and with a bourgeoisie whose taste was a rehash of this previous grandomania of older ruling classes.

The American travellers, in their bouts with this architecture, were goaded on by social ambition and photography. Confused by the heterogeneous architectural assortment, they chose from any European style they thought was a winner—like sticking a pin in a racing card—with the idea of impressing the folks back home. Travel showed the wives of the magnates just how Dorothy Vernon kept Haddon Hall, and the kind of draperies used by Marie Antoinette. Photography made it possible to bring back accurate records of all this. In fact, it laid the entire architectural repertoire of the past right on their grand pianos.

There seems to be no other reasonable explanation for George Vanderbilt's Gothic château in North Carolina, Mrs. Hugh Dillman's Spanish hacienda in Palm Beach, and Barnum's Persian villa at Bridgeport.

Most of the architects employed by the American millionaires had received their training from one school—the Ecole des Beaux Arts in Paris, the architectural section of which was started in 1818. The students were surrounded by "collections of mouldings of the Middle Ages and the Renaissance," and copies of paintings which each pensioner of the Academy of France at Rome was obliged to send to the school.

The principal aim of the Ecole des Beaux Arts seems to have been to re-establish the tradition of the Middle Ages and the Renaissance, but Roman and Greek temples, thermae, and mausoleums were also considered ideal subjects for plagiarism.

One of the most famous of the Beaux Arts architectural firms in America was McKim, Mead and White, which, early in the century, built the Sherry Restaurant, Madison Square Garden, and the Vanderbilt residence at Hyde Park, New York—all naturally in different historical styles.

Stanford White was the dominant partner, and his guiding belief was that all good design stemmed from Europe, a belief in which he joined hot hands with the cognoscenti of his day. The fact that he had copied the Giralda Tower from Seville's cathedral to house horse shows and prize fights at Madison Square Garden, did not strike him as at all odd. Nor was it a sense of humor that prompted his firm to house the Vanderbilts in a stone-built travesty of Buckingham Palace at Hyde Park, New York.

Stanford White's idea of a cosy American pied-à-terre was the house he put together for William C. Whitney, formerly at 871 Fifth Avenue, New York City. The entrance hall (which must have been something to walk into after a bicycle tea at Claremont) looked like a combination of the tapestry department at Wanamaker's and the lower level of Grand Central Station. There were tapestries lapping the stone stairs, tapestries draped as portieres, and tapestries cut up as pillows on the red velvet sofas.

If the dining room, with its coffered ceiling, Renaissance stone fireplace, and table scarf and chairs in Genoese velvet had more than a taste of Nesselrode pudding, the drawing room, with its distinct cornstarch and Louis XV flavor, was the spot where McKim, Mead and White really went to town. This enormous room was festooned with luscious French furbishings, as though one had bought Versailles from a dry goods store by the bolt, and just draped it from floor to ceiling. It was unique until the entrance hall at the Hollywood Theatre outshone it, and dazzled Broadway a few years later.

On a warm June day in 1906, the activities of Stanford White came to an end when he was shot and instantly killed by Harry K. Thaw. This over-hasty gesture was not an indication, however, that Mr. Thaw had any preferences in architecture—Beaux Arts or otherwise.

"Let every young Beaux Arts man take courage today. There is a place for him and he need not even seek it for it will seek him if only he works hard and does good work," said Thomas Hastings, a leading architect of the early 1900's. This rosy prognosis was only too true because all over residential New York, in the long lines of brownstone façades, gaps were appearing, which were soon filled with "palatial" French, Gothic, Romanesque, Italian, and English residences. These were in the best style of the Beaux Arts boys, who had been sought out to some purpose by the Astors, the Schieffelins, the Whitneys, and others of the multiplying readers of the Almanach de Gotha.

Fifth Avenue was aflower with top-heavy, variegated architectural blooms from the seed packets brought over from Paris. The furniture wagons were standing on the sidewalks, being emptied of French, Italian, and Spanish Renaissance furniture,

Wurlitzer organs, and a great deal of upholstery designed in a manner beggaring even the most erudite background to describe. The horse troughs, even, had become rococo.

While this architectural carnival was getting up steam in America, the first protests were being voiced in London, where it had been going on for some time. A certain Mr. Owen Jones, with a passion worthy of his Druidical descent, had this to say: "We go from bad to worse; from the Gothic mania we fell into the Elizabethan. . . . We have had an Italian mania, and we are threatened with a Renaissance mania from France. It would be unfortunate . . . if the Great Exhibition should result in an Indian one.

"The fault lies with the public: the public must educate themselves on this subject. Architects unfortunately can but obey their clients; this one will have an Elizabethan mansion; this clergyman . . . a mediaeval church; this railway director has a fancy for a Moorish tunnel or Doric termini . . . an Egyptian suspension bridge. The worst I ever saw was an engine house in facsimile of a mosque. The minaret was the chimney shaft. . . . We must be up and stirring if we would not that England, in the midst of her material greatness, become a byword and a reproach amongst nations."

Mr. Owen Jones had little effect in England, and none in America, where Gothic colleges, Renaissance police stations, Moorish temples, Greek courthouses and depots were multiplying like the imported English sparrows.

In 1900, Louis Sullivan, who had cracked down on the Chicago Fair, was up and stirring again, and, having looked with dismay at the cluttering architectural monstrosities around him, spoke his piece.

"American architecture," he despaired, "is composed, in the

In the brownstone façades the gaping spaces were soon filled

hundred, of ninety parts aberration, eight parts indifference, one part poverty and one part Little Lord Fauntleroy. You can have the prescription filled at any architectural department store, or select architectural millinery establishment.

"Yet there is a certain grim ghastly humor in it all; for instance: —a banker sitting in a Roman temple . . . a Wall Street broker living in a French château; a rich vulgarian living in a Trianon; a modern person living in a Norman castle."

The department store and millinery establishment referred to was really the Ecole des Beaux Arts, at which the Vanderbilts, the Goelets, the Belmonts, and the Whitneys were such good cash customers. But Mr. Sullivan was too tactful to say so outright.

Just what confections the John-Frederics of that day were dreaming up is beyond me, but no milliner in his wackiest concoctions could have sewn together anything to equal one of the 1900 architectural day-dreams—the New York Yacht Club. No girl, even to attend the opening night of the ballet today, ever cooked up anything quite like this architectural toque, with its carved stone aigrettes and mousseline de soie grotto work.

Most of the architectural millinery of the period has disappeared, and some day the Yacht Club will go too. When that day comes, the temptation to save it as a Tunnel of Love, with the boats going clear through to Forty-fifth Street, will be irresistible.

If there were others besides Louis Sullivan who saw what a bitter aftertaste would follow this Beaux Arts binge, their voices were unheard. There is a faint protest from Sullivan's pupil, Frank Lloyd Wright, who said, "I've been too close to Mr. Sullivan. He has helped spoil the Beaux Arts for me, or spoiled me for the Beaux Arts I guess I mean."

Mr. Wright was to learn to thunder much stronger views at a later date.

While New York and the big cities were in a fever of antiquity, down under the palm trees Florida crackers had the surprise of their lives coming to them. The first World War had put an end to the French Riviera and "dear old Monte," and millionaires were coming into their peaceful swamps to bring untold amazement to the Seminoles by their gaudy cavortings.

Palm Beach was the last big production number of the Gilded Age. Just as the film spectacles of Cecil B. de Mille and the stage spectacles of Belasco and Reinhardt marked the end of an era of extravagant theatrical realism, so Palm Beach was to be the grand finale of the equivalent theatricality in architecture.

The story of the aggrandizement of Palm Beach is the story of one man. The next rainy afternoon that comes along, I want you to pick up an overweight volume called the *Florida Architecture of Addison Mizner,* with an introduction by Ida M. Tarbell, and read of the winter days of Drexel Biddle Jr., Edward T. Stotesbury, Harold Vanderbilt, and Rodman Wanamaker. Meanwhile, for all of you who want an antidote to the war news, here is Palm Beach in powder form. All you have to do is add your own boiling water.

Addison Mizner was the Maestro who put on the Palm Beach follies, and Ida Tarbell his Boswell. Mizner was born in California in 1872, adored his mother, whom he called "Mamma Mizner," and "dreamed all his life of building her a cathedral," a childish whim it might be well to bear in mind, by the way, as a clue to later goings-on.

The Mizner clan next appeared in Guatemala, where Addison was enthralled with convents, monasteries and haciendas, and resolved to become an architect. To this end he was sent to the University in Salamanca, Spain, where "surrounded by the accumulation of centuries of beautiful creations, the collector Mizner seems to have been born."

"It would be a hard thing," he admitted later, "for me to pick out even a short list of the really fine things that I have brought to America, for I have looted cathedrals, churches, and palaces, and brought a shipload or two of everything from stone doorways to fine laces from both Central America and Europe."

In this stark admission, we see very clearly how far the confusion had gone between what was architecture and what were the activities of an out-of-town antique buyer on Third Avenue— a confusion that existed not only in the minds of men like Mizner, but also in the minds of his clients, particularly those in Palm Beach.

Meanwhile, to continue the saga, we read that after two years in Alaska, where "whatever there was of the snob in him died," he moved on again, "and after a dip in the Orient, perhaps to take the taste of too much Alaska out of his mouth, he settled in New York."

In 1918, he arrived in Palm Beach. He had brought with him his notebooks filled with sketches of Spanish architecture, and with this stock in trade, he decided with appallingly misplaced enthusiasm to turn the mangrove swamps into a conglomeration of this Spanish memorabilia. Here is the clue, in his own words, to the way he proposed to realize his fond dream:

"Most modern architects have spent their lives carrying out a period to the last letter, and producing a characterless copybook effect. My ambition has been to take the reverse stand—to make a building look traditional and as though it had fought its way from a small unimportant structure to a great rambling house that took centuries of different needs and ups and downs of wealth to accomplish. I sometimes start a house with a Romanesque corner, pretend that it has fallen in disrepair, and been added to in the Gothic spirit, when suddenly the great wealth of the New World has poured in and the owner added a very rich Renaissance addition."

All of which is so much architectural baloney, because however you mix up Romanesque corners, Gothic spirit, and Renaissance additions, the final result is still a copybook effect that has nothing to do with the landscape, or the climate of Florida, and still less to do with imagination or contemporary design, and nothing at all to do with America.

Addison Mizner's Gothic spirit, by the way, is of such potency that in the main entrance hall of the Hugh Dillman hacienda it has positively inebriated the architecture. The result is a bacchanalia of swirling columns, flying staircases, and vaulted ceilings. Even a "rich Renaissance addition" would have very little calming effect on it.

Palm Beach today looks very much like one of the lots outside a Hollywood studio, seen, of course, from the view of the camera. It also bears a striking resemblance to the Roxy Theatre. It has a dated look. A thoughtful visitor, lingering in one of the self-conscious patios, with the oil jars placed artfully in odd corners, or dining under a faked antique coffered ceiling from a faked refectory table, must feel that far from being in the atmosphere of ancient Spain, he is merely back in the 1920's, with President Coolidge, "Gentlemen Prefer Blondes," bobbed hair, the Dolly Sisters—and—Addison Mizner.

Let's go, Amigos!

6. LADIES' DAY

"You shall no longer take things at second or third hand, nor look through the eyes of the dead, nor feed on the spectres in the books."

W A L T   W H I T M A N

THE words "interior decorating" today bring a mental picture of busy people running around with a pick-me-up for wilting upholstery, and scouring Third Avenue for "something amusing and chic"—all for ten per cent profit. But there was a time when the cognoscenti regarded as gospel the words of the top-drawer interior decorators.

The tragic incident, recounted in Elsie de Wolfe's book, of the misguided woman who boasted: "This is my Louis XVI ballroom," and received the reply: "What makes you think so?," was not just a funny story. It was a warning of the humiliation that awaited other foolish women who thought they knew better than interior decorators.

As time went on, the public got wise to the important difference between real Louis XVI and bastard Louis XVI, knew a bergère chair when they saw one, and remembered to say "chaise longue" instead of "parlor lounge." It then became necessary to introduce new fashions in antiques and interior decorating, in order to keep the hostesses and their houses on tip-toe, as well as in their proper place as mere uninformed non-professionals.

Sometimes these new styles were launched via a book, sometimes by many words of many mouths, more often in magazine articles. But launched they were. In the early days the changes were slow, but as competition in interior decorating increased, many a society girl was caught with three hundred thousand dollars' worth of Elizabethan house on her hands, only to discover a Spanish hacienda was *de rigueur* with her less hasty

[43]

friends and enemies. There are records of women, who shall be nameless of course, who built and discarded as many as five houses before catching up with the latest taste of the beau monde and the approval of the socially powerful interior decorators.

The more cautious finally arrived at a safe compromise by having a library in English oak, a drawing-room in a French style, a dining-room in Georgian, and a hall in Gothic or Renaissance. The interior decorators considered this hitting below the belt, since the crabbing that went on among them, as each worked out his specialty under the same roof, revealed cherished trade secrets to Fifth Avenue chatelaines. To these ladies, however, this was a soothing revenge for being snubbed by the haughty business queens of décor.

The story of how the fashionable changes were rung on the antique repertoire is an engaging epic, deserving of a more detailed recording than this book will allow; but even a rough outline has its moments, and here they are, beginning with that much abused expression, "the turn of the century."

It was just at this time, when Stanford White's dreary Italian and other period architecture was turning sour, that Elsie de Wolfe led off with Louis XVI, and retrimmed the whole antiquana in chintz and toile de Jouy. This shot in the upholstery kept antiques alive for a time, then they drooped again.

In 1916, Ruby Ross Wood took a slug at the phlegmatic antique world by painting the street floor of her house on Eleventh Street bright pink. She followed this up by introducing modern wallpapers and bright colors as backgrounds for antique furniture, in contrast with the painted *boiserie* and paler Edwardian coloring previously used by Elsie de Wolfe. Under this girlish stimulation the grim period rooms loosened up their stays a little, while boudoirs and bedrooms took them off altogether and just relaxed.

This was the beginning of what proved a field day for fabric, wallpaper, and carpet houses, which could now sell gaudier and gayer merchandise to the interior decorators bent on revitalizing their antique furniture formula. It was also the beginning of a boom in amateur interior decoration, when every woman was running around the corner to some "little man" and doing her own "fixing over." This flurry kept antiques going very nicely. Then, in 1925, the girls once again began to grow restless, when Paris staged the Exposition of Decorative Arts, and talk of "modern" furniture began to creep into the antique chatter. In fact, things got so bad it began to look as if they had almost forgotten the genteel up-bringing of Elsie de Wolfe.

It was none other than Mrs. Price Post, better known as "Emily," who brought them smartly to order with a book called *The Personality of a House, or The Blue Book of Home Design and Decoration,* published in 1930. To future historians groping around for a clue to the architectural and decorative chaos of America in the 1930's, I heartily recommend a copy of this book by Emily Post, since it must have done as much to foment this chaos as *Uncle Tom's Cabin* helped to foment the Civil War.

Mrs. Post suggests a complete gamut of past historical styles for American houses. Tudor, Italian, Spanish, Jacobean, Georgian, French are all recommended for the family; Elizabethan, Spanish or Georgian for bachelors. The illustrations lean toward a genteel version of pseudo-Colonial-cum-French Provincial interiors with spinning-wheels, rush-bottomed spindle-backed chairs, "quaint chintzes," and the general air of marigolds-in-pewter-tankards that has now become the formula for Colonial tea shoppes. In an effort to pep up this limited, rather cautious historical refinement, Mrs. Post throws in a chapter of "portrait interiors," including "a boudoir for an exotic beauty," and one on "backgrounds for blondes."

"Let it not be said that this book is mid-Victorian," she says, plunging into this exotic come-on with the air of a tipsy dowager doing the bumps on New Year's Eve. After warning her readers that a "boudoir is *not* a bedroom," she blushes on into the appalling description of the exotic beauty: "fragilely thin, white skinned, with red-gold copper colored hair . . . languid, exquisite and utterly sophisticated."

The walls framing this Elinor Glyn heroine are "highly polished black glass . . . the ceiling is, of course, silver. The window has glass curtains of orchid chiffon, and heavy curtains of magenta satin. The carpet would be black, and the mantel of green veined black marble. A broad divan covered with jade green velvet should be set in a recess of engraved mirrors, and a dozen very large square box-edged plain satin cushions in flesh, orchid, magenta, and deep black-purple should be packed too tight to slip against the mirror-back and sides." All of which, you must admit, is as nice a variation on quaint chintzes as you will find this side of certain unphotographed "boudoirs" in Panama City.

The chapter that follows this is a house for "the stay-at-home mother." It is "big and rambling and Elizabethan in type," and gives Mrs. Post time to rinse her pen in Listerine and cool off generally before limbering up again in "backgrounds for blondes."

There are apparently three types, in the world of Mrs. Post: "Noonday blondes," "moon blondes," and "drab blondes"; but there are *no* peroxide blondes. In fact, the noondays, moons and drabs are damned refined girls after all, especially the drab, who is the "most essentially thoroughbred," and "fits into the sort of house that a man likes with the suitability of a boy," whatever that may mean.

After such sections as "Rooms That Are Bad Mannered," "Occult Balance," "As the Elizabethan Period Applies to Us," "The Spanish Versus the Italian Personality," "The Magic Digestion of the Renaissance," and "Windows Are the Smiles of a House," Mrs. Post whets her knife and stalks in for the killing in the last chapter called, "The Style We Know as Modern."

As I said before, America was feeling the effects of the Paris Exposition. The girls were getting into their heads ideas which threatened to undermine all the refined pseudo-historical background from which Mrs. Post issued her edicts on living. Much, therefore, depended on her ability to show them the error of their ways.

Since already there were hints that the antique styles were dead, Mrs. Post decided to hurl this heresy back with interest. She described the creations of moderns as "deathlike," with their "rounded edges of highly polished, massively plain rectangles of ebon darkness suggestive of coffins." Modern beds were "all too often a catafalque." These, together with "coffin sideboards," "crypts built into the walls," and other suggestions "of cemetery monuments and mortuary chambers," were the beginning of an "aesthetic decline" which is also "a circus ring," "an asylum for the insane," and a "quest for newness" that is "fanatical."

"Modern design," writes Mrs. E. P., pale with fury, ". . . does not fit in with the traditions that many of us are *hampered by* (italics mine). One value of old furniture is that quite inevitably it imparts the quality of ancestry; one fault of the modern interior is that quite as inevitably it flaunts the fact that it has none. . . . Perhaps many of us care nothing for inherited traditions. Very well! And yet—without any, what are we? Nameless, familyless—born in the foundling asylum?"

This must have scared the daylights out of the girls, and sent them scampering back into the houses of their Jacobean, Georgian, Colonial, and French "ancestors," while timid bachelors scurried back to their Elizabethan and Spanish hangouts, which had been there presumably since the Armada.

Mrs. Post, exhausted finally with all this vituperation and unladylike scolding, and a little baffled by the movement to create a contemporary style in place of the nice fool-proof formula of antiques, admits: "At all events, the estimate of Modern style is rather a hopeless puzzle to solve."

Nevertheless, the effect of this book, with its cozy reassurance that "mother knows best," put the antiques on their claw and ball feet once again. But not for long.

Perhaps it was a result of the depression—I don't know—anyway, antiques started to slip once more. This time the girls were just plain listless. Decoration and furniture were a crashing bore. Business—antique business—was at its wit's end.

Through the darkness came Mrs. Syrie Maugham.

Syrie was the wife of Somerset Maugham, the novelist, and what her husband did for the outposts of Empire, Mrs. Syrie Maugham did for antiques. She made them glamorous again.

In 1882, Oscar Wilde had said to Americans: "You have too many white walls." And for the next fifty years, walls were colored to high heaven. The secret of Mrs. Maugham's adrenalin for antiques was that everything around them went white again almost overnight. It was like waking up and looking for the old familiar things in the parlor, and finding instead a snowscape, or a whitescape.

Vogue pounced on it. "Mrs. Syrie Maugham—that famous

Le Touquet house of hers, which really set the fashion for the new type of décor." Her London house: "Bare white plaster walls, furniture done up in whitewash satin and brocade, silver curtains, a white rug by Marion Dorn, flaring white peacock feathers. The only color in the living room of the first lady of white is in the two dramatic negro heads near the feathers on the console tables."

The "first lady of white" was riding high, and soon *House and Garden* was showing pictures of a Syrie Maugham white drawing room at the New York home of Mr. and Mrs. Harrison Williams, in which "the various furnishings blend and are contrasted with the white walls. White as demonstrated here," says *House and Garden* rather cautiously, "is capable of many tones and relationships."

The rejuvenescence of the Chippendale furniture of no less a person than Mrs. Harrison Williams was heady stuff, and America whitewashed to a woman, peacock feathers or no peacock feathers, in homage to such glamorous leadership.

Now things were quiet once more, and if inside their ashen surroundings the girls heard the decoration newsboys yelling, "Extree! Extree! Swedish Modern and Regency on Fifty-seventh Street! Readallaboutit," they kept mum, and toyed with a stag's head in white plaster, and concentrated on Mrs. Harrison Williams.

Something was just bound to happen sooner or later. By the time the white damask had turned a tattle-tale gray, and the ruching was flattened to a pancake, along came Dorothy Draper with a preface by Mrs. Theodore Roosevelt, Jr. Mrs. Tuckerman Draper, to give her name in full, had a new one—"Decorating," she said, "is Fun!"

Now decoration had been a lot of things before this, it's true.

It had been: "antiques in chintz," "antiques in bright colors," "antiques that took the curse of 'foundling' from you," "antiques in white," and just plain "antiques." But never before had antiques been "fun." Once again the girls were agog.

When I tell you that on page 14 of Mrs. Draper's book there is a case history of a Mrs. Valentine, with a room of "white walls, a white floor, and a big modern off-white rug," and a Mr. Valentine who is white with rage at this mistaken idea of chic, and "goes to his club now much more than he used to," you will get an idea of the way the new hilarity was leading. The laugh was on Mrs. Maugham.

Says Mrs. Draper: "Try to picture to yourself (grab your head in your hands like a Shakespearean actor if you want) a cyclamen in the sunshine—the leaf of a lily of the valley . . . the darkly shimmering greens on the back of a frog . . . Try the same technique on a room but go more slowly here, stopping after each new step so that the colors are glowing firmly in your mind."

At this point, a million or so women, grabbing their heads in as many corny attitudes, turned their backs heartlessly on Mrs. Syrie Maugham and society leaders, and concentrated on the back of a frog instead. Or am I getting this whole damn thing backwards? Perhaps it's the room that they grab. What's the difference? It's fun we're after, and this is nothing less than hysterical. Try it yourself. You'll be in stitches.

"We jumble our periods cheerfully," says Mrs. Draper, presumably holding her sides at the thought of it all. Amongst the periods suggested for this decorative junket are Georgian, Regency, Early Colonial, French Provincial, English, Tudor, and a soupçon of Baroque.

As Emily Post did twenty years before her, Mrs. Draper includes a suggestion for a man's bedroom. At this point one cannot escape the feeling that the ladies have much in common, twenty years of solid progress notwithstanding. Both are four-square Anglophiles when it comes to housing male virility. A man's room should be Elizabethan, according to Emily Post, a somewhat trite suggestion compared to the subtlety of Mrs. Draper, who puts her men in a bedroom with walls of "dark London fog," and lamps made from "old-fashioned brass spittoons."

This suggestion of deep calling to deep occurs again in "Decorating Is Fun!", in a passage entitled "A Sophisticated Living Room." This pseudo-sexy mise en scène is inhabited by an owner with "a mass of red hair . . . a glowing white skin and bright red lips"—a curious resemblance, one might add, to the exotic beauty previously invoked by Emily Post.

There are differences, however, in the furnishings. I notice that Mrs. Post's sybarite reclines on a divan of green, flesh, orchid, magenta and purple black, while Mrs. Draper's apparition favors a "hassock at least four feet in diameter, covered in black and white civet cat fur."

Personally, I'm for Fifth Avenue Chippendale and whitewash by Syrie Maugham!

7. MADAME,
YOUR ANTIQUES ARE SHOWING

"The selling campaign of the bogus antique was remarkably well managed through skilful publicity and propaganda, by those who were first to see its commercial possibilities. . . .

"Thus did the virus of a culture, snobbish and alien to the land, perform its work of disintegration . . . a culture lost in ghostly mesalliance with abstractions, when what the world needs is courage, common sense, and human sympathy, and a moral standard that is plain, valid and livable."

LOUIS SULLIVAN

THE flagrant story of antique furniture propaganda and its effect on American taste is one that never has been fully explored. Personally, I'd be for keeping away from it and not inviting calenture of the brain; on the other hand, we must steel ourselves for at least a look-in on part of this blood-curdling process.

To begin at the beginning: some poor kid starts out to learn interior decorating, and pays good money for being taught a sketchy outline of period furniture with a footnote added about something called "modern," which according to these schools is a kind of manicured antique style.

Vogue, that sounding board of tinkling symbols, reports that Mr. Van Day Truex, the head of the Parsons School of Design in New York, has decorated his apartment with "space-cheating mirrors on either side of a black-fringed mantel. And in the Victorian manner, he stuffed the rooms with furniture—with whimsies and fine pieces—junk-shop gilt chairs, two Empire tables."

I know one instance of an intrepid pupil at one of these fountainheads of décor who said she wanted to study contemporary furniture, and was told to draw a Louis XVI room and then simplify it. When she questioned whether Louis XVI and contemporary were synonymous, she was told to go and study the collection of Venetian furniture owned by the boss himself. That squelched her!

Eventually the kid gets a job with a decorator. She waits until she knows the clientele, and then hangs up her own shingle and decorates, which means filling one or a series of rooms with antiques and semi-antiques. Then the magazines photograph from all angles, and add such hair-raising captions as "She Dotes on Ruffles and Frills," "Decorator Uses French Provincial," "A Game Room to Stir the Romantic Urge," "Romantic Trend— Regency and Victorian." And on and on *ad nauseam*.

Now Grand Rapids takes up the ball—or the romantic trend. And it's no trend any more, believe me, when Victorian and Regency roll off the assembly lines. It's the Crystal Palace and the Brighton Pavilion from coast to coast.

Then it's the turn of the department store furniture buyers to take a jaunt to the Grand Rapids Furniture Mart at Chicago. They have read the magazines, and know that a million readers of "The House Nifty" are now waiting for Victorian and Regency to satisfy their romantic yearnings. It isn't very long before hundreds of department stores are showing cute Regency corners and Victorian nooks, and brides are being led to the kill by "mom," who loves a bit of the romantic, even if it is at second hand.

And the kid who became an interior decorator is now getting worried because it isn't chic to use Victorian or Regency any more, and every period seems to have been squeezed dry.

More responsible than anything else for bringing all this on are the magazines—women's magazines, fashion magazines, and home furnishings magazines—which have had the American house foremost on their sucker list for the last fifty years.

She dotes on ruffles and frills

The fact that a few châteaux were built on Fifth Avenue, and a few of the clients of fashionable interior decorators preferred to live *à la française* is not important. What is important is that through the magazines this snobbish preoccupation with antiques filters into every section of the community, until it becomes the superstition of people who wouldn't recognize a French château if they saw one, and who have never met an interior decorator in their lives. From the late 1800's, when antique furniture first got its teeth into America, the magazines have lashed their decoration-drunk followers to a state of complete befuddlement and exhaustion. They have sponsored over the last fifty years at least sixty different "period" styles—an average of more than one a year. God knows, it must be tough going to whip up new decoration ideas once a month, with one baleful eye on the Grand Rapids advertisers, and one straining ear to the ground, listening for the drum-beats of fashionable decorators along Fifty-seventh Street. But even so, the proud record of utter confusion has remained unsullied and without a speck of good common sense to mar its ga-ga-ity.

These magazines have driven the housewives of America from attic to cellar in an agitation of "fixing over" that would curdle the blood of more sober *Frauen* elsewhere. But worse than this, they have driven the Grand Rapids furniture manufacturers deeper and deeper into the antique furniture quagmire. The furniture magazines, the interior decorators, the interior-decorating schools, and the house-furnishings sections of department stores have run a neck-and-neck race, on which the women of America have laid good money and never been paid off. This quartet has bamboozled millions of women into constantly changing their furnishings to absolutely no purpose, since in their combined careers they have not produced any furniture which could be remotely described as contemporary in design, or, more important, as completely American.

Starting from the Italian macaroni days of Stanford White, and the French pastry of Elsie de Wolfe, every possible variation of the antique menu has been scooped in and gobbled up. It is already years since Victorian was dished out, after which, according to sober aesthetes, the jig was up. But they had underestimated those pixie folk of *The House Gorgeous* and *Art and the Hearth.* Victorian led gaily on to Early-Edwardian and Late-Edwardian, to say nothing of cutie-pie adaptations of cast-iron stoves and discarded benches from Gramercy Park. When *House and Garden* talks of "an original piece signed by Belter, the great Victorian designer," who knows what breath-taking discoveries remain unrevealed in other fields of mediocrity?

At any moment housewives in the Bronx and brides in Toledo will turn the shining pages of the latest edition of *Girlette,* and find that the three-piece suite from the mail-order catalogue is the newest "period," and they must hold on to it until the fifteenth of next month, after which, God help them, they are on their own again.

Naturally, one cannot speak of the fifteenth of the month without a mention of the fashion magazines, particularly the matriarch, *Vogue.* In the late 1800's, *Vogue* was in love with European high life, and followed the triumphs and failures of Americans in and around it with the joy and anxiety of unabashed snobbism. As well as recording in those early days such titbits as the fact that Mr. Ward McAllister was seen sitting in the Savoy with "one duchess, a dozen lords or so and a few correctly dressed Guardsmen," *Vogue,* from its inauguration over fifty years ago, has advocated collecting antiques. Its attitude in

1895 was that the spick-and-span newness of living American designers was "outmoded," as we see in an article of the April issue of that year. "The craze for antiques and furniture of Colonial times has had its origin in this generation, for the one preceding it in this country had no taste or inclination for anything that was not spick-and-span new." After describing the spick-and-span taste of what it calls "our dear mothers," the article goes on to say: "It was only when communication with Europe became more frequent and Americans began to spend their summers in wandering through old palaces and castles on the other side, that our women awakened to the enormous blunder they had made. Then began the hunt for old 'bits' and pieces so recently despised.

"Farmers' wives were startled by visits from richly dressed ladies in search of spinning wheels, brass andirons and coal-scuttles, and much admiration was lavished upon the antique writing desks and chests of drawers.

"Since then the demand for these things has increased so enormously year by year that all modern furniture is manufactured in imitation of them, though the imitations are sadly inferior to the originals."

Vogue, during its long career, also has had a yearning for the whimsical, and in the same article it offers this cute tip, which is the forerunner of a long progeny of similar misguided ingenuity: "Handsomely carved bedposts are now detached from the bedstead and mounted on substantial mahogany stands with brass hooks for ladies' dressing rooms."

A whimsey for bric-a-brac was, of course, all a part of *Vogue's* passion for European high life, where the collecting fad was well under way. In 1895, we find *Vogue's* Paris correspondent bringing this thrilling news to American readers: "The mania of Parisian great ladies for bric-a-brac is assuming gigantic proportions. Every one of our 'mondaines' is following in this respect the leaders of fashion.

"The Comtesse de Chambrun has left, among other relics, a buskin of Mlle Rachel, the celebrated tragedienne. . . . This is nothing, however, to the extraordinary collection of Princess Yousoupoff (Comtesse Chauvan) . . . the Princess had spent years of her life in buying hundreds of warming pans, including one that belonged to Madame de Pompadour, one of Marie Leczinska, and one of the Empress Catherine of Russia, valued at the rather staggering figure of $3,000.00.

"The grand genre is to possess some unique piece and to exhibit it—negligently—in one's drawing room or boudoir. I saw the other day a chocolatière or chocolate pot once the property of the Roi Soleil (Louis XIV) wherein six or seven lilies of the valley grew unconcernedly."

When Royal Princesses were spending years looking for the discarded warming pans of near-royal tramps and defunct queens, to say nothing of a buskin or two, and a chocolate pot, it behove the richly dressed ladies of America to get busy and whip up a spinning wheel, or better still, a coal scuttle, or be scuttled themselves, at least as far as the "grand genre" was concerned.

After decades of this type of dégagé rubbernecking, with an occasional skittish ogle for fun, *Vogue* tangled with surrealism and the new mode of slumming for décor. Gone were the days of Elsie de Wolfe and Trianon Villas. Gone even were the moments of best-dressed women and their eighteenth-century mahogany and of Syrie Maugham with chic buckets of whitewash.

In their place was Third Avenue, Tchelitchew and Salvador Dali, to say nothing of Diana Vreeland, whose whirling-dervish fantasies were becoming a feature of the interior decoration pages in the rival magazine, *Harper's Bazaar*.

After brooding over this changing world, and dropping darkling threats about the "honest beauty of old glossy-as-chestnut antiques, outlasting many ephemeral fads," *Vogue* decided to get in on the clambake, forget its gloomy forebodings, and be as hell-hot for antique catnip as the next girl (the next girl being, I suspect, Madame Vreeland).

With a prayer on its caption—"God Bless Our Home"—*Vogue* went in with its type blazing. "Clutter the place up," it yelled. "Paper the walls *and* piano in a bright figured paper," adding the rather vicious aside, "It can be scraped later at great expense." "Use Victorian bow-knots in royal blue, with furniture (from obscure second-hand shops) painted in black and white. . . . Your terrace . . . go into the country and find a second-hand shop . . . the kind of place that sells to boarding-houses . . . buy Edwardian suites . . . upholster in bright pink or yellow. For a small dining room . . . use kitchen furniture . . . from a junk shop, a bulbous ornate old-fashioned stove. . . . Your hall . . . a Victorian mirror . . . surround it with black cast-iron hooks to hang your overcoats on and try a couple of bowler hats. They should be most decorative."

While wrought up to this hallelujah for the second-hand, boarding-houses, and junk shops, it was obviously only by sheer effort of will that *Vogue* resisted the temptation to run amuck and tell its readers that for the truly grand chic you couldn't beat a flop house in the Bowery. Personally, I question whether all these rummage-sale romps had any telling effect on the manifestoes issued at steady intervals by *Harper's Bazaar*, in which Diana Vreeland reached heights of decorative phantasmagoria apparently beyond the reach of the sister magazine.

In *Harper's* fiery furnace of trivia, antique and semi-antique furniture was melted into new frothy forms undreamed of elsewhere. It was to this deep well of consciousness that the beau monde hurried in its breathless search for the ultimate in decoration. On a sticky July day in 1937, they found Diana Vreeland advising: "If you are tired of your pine farmhouse furniture, paint it white picked out with gold, and with red satin ribbons tie little cushions of leopard plush on the chair seats." There was further urgent advice for the jaded antique lovers, who were implored "to raise Japanese cherry trees, or white lilac trees, and put them around the bed against brown Coromandel screens."

"Why don't you," she continued to urge in throbbing phrases, "revive the old-fashioned hat tree—this time a white lacquer pole topped with ostrich feathers . . . or a black and gold palm tree—most useful in a bathroom to hold your clothes."

After reading several of these fragile epistles, one is able to piece together a day in the life of a woman of that forgotten period—a day, one might say, as revealed by the rediscovered *belles-lettres* of Diana Vreeland, written in 1937 along these lines:

It is high noon. The beau monde stirs from its sleep (the Dead End kids, of course, have been up for hours), and our heroine stirs too, as well she might. There is quite a day ahead.

Reluctantly she throws back the "white monkey fur bedcover mounted on yellow velvet," and reaches for a cigarette in an "English ram's head, mounted with silver." This isn't as simple as it sounds, because the ram's head is in a "plain pine knife-basket with two compartments and a handle," used as a bedside table.

Brushing back the branches of the trees growing around the bed, she puffs away moodily and peers through the underbrush. Then as a thought strikes her, she crawls out under a torrential shower of Japanese cherry blossoms (and probably Japanese beetles, too).

While she is still on all fours, we see she is wearing a "supremely smart Vionnet negligée of black and pink polka-dotted silk," the entire outfit torn to ribbons by her advance through the cherry trees.

Straightening up and brushing off the last blossom, she looks at the bedroom with its "enormous bay window with broderie anglaise dyed bright green and held here and there with black pailletted butterflies." The bed, of which only the top is showing over the cherry trees, is a "tent bed of bamboo . . . with a gossamer drapery of white cotton voile printed in enormous pink and red roses."

Our heroine glances up at "an eighteenth-century clock made like a birdcage. On the hour the bird sings." At this second, it bursts into a lusty rendering of the Carmagnole, meaning it is getting very late. So skirting around a "ladder-backed chair, completely trellised over with artificial waxed ivy leaves," she vanishes in a puff of pink polka-dotted butterflies.

The lovely laughing girl is next seen in the living room designed to look like Mae West (and if you think I'm kidding, you're crazy). "The stairs make an 1890 dog collar, the mouth is a red divan, her nose the fireplace, her eyes are two Dali surrealist paintings, her hair and earrings, draperies."

With a fine disregard of sanity, dream girl sits on the mouth,

*and puts a light to the nose (it is February 1938, and chilly),
then settling well into the upper lip, she pats a Peruvian cavy
with long silky hair growing in rosettes. She listens to the crackle
of the logs in the nostrils. She is dreaming of the March issue
of* Harper's Bazaar, *and is in touch with Eternity.*

8. GOING–GOING–GONE

"In art, democracy means that some thought of your own, some feeling you have about the thing yourself, should enter into everything you have to do, so that everything you have may be your own and everything you do be sincerely yourself. Democracy in this true sense is really the highest form of aristocracy the world has ever known. The aristocracy of qualities, not of birth or circumstances. . . . Slaves of fashion, human sheep, are the curse of this ideal; relics of an aristocracy that was an imposition and now is passing in anguish."

FRANK LLOYD WRIGHT

READERS of the *New York Times*, glancing through its crisp pages on February 26, 1943, must have put their coffee cups down with more than a clatter, as they ran head on into this morsel of news:

"Decorators confide that the days of plush and fanfare, though numbered, are not yet ended. Stocks still on hand in this store and others will provide a formal parlor if that is the order. As testimony, Sloane's offers another completely refurnished room— or more accurately, parlor—in the Victorian mode."

This reassurance that Victorian parlors were still available in 1943—that more days of plush and fanfare still lay ahead—was made on the occasion of the hundredth anniversary of W. & J. Sloane, the Fifth Avenue furniture store. To those familiar with the ways of the New York furniture world, there was nothing odd in celebrating a century of dogged progress by exhibiting a Victorian parlor. On the contrary, it was inevitable that such a moment *would* be chosen to give further reassurance that time can still be halted dead in its tracks by undaunted decorators; though, mind you, even they are fearful that the days of such goings-on, alas, are numbered.

Far be it from me to cast a gloom over this brave Indian summer of the decorating and antique world, but, strictly for the record, we might take note of these last carefree hours, and count the straws in the cooling wind.

The first wisp blew in one January day in 1941. It was announced that part of the collection of William Randolph Hearst was to go under the hammer. This in itself was not unduly alarming; big collections of antique furniture are always being auctioned off somewhere in the world. What made the Hearst sale significant was the place chosen for its dispersal— Gimbel's department store. This was a strange departure from the great traditions of important antique auctioneering that had been established over a century ago by Christie's in London. And it was rightly viewed in real alarm by the antique dealers and interior decorators, quite apart from the fact that the sudden dumping of millions of dollars' worth of antique curiosa might have appalling results on its hitherto carefully guarded prestige and value.

This collection had been highly publicized. It was almost a part of American legend—a fabulous treasure-trove stored in warehouses on 143rd Street, New York City, until Mr. Hearst called from San Simeon for some suit of armor, or panelled room, or an odd monastery at the odd moment. In the palmy days, whole liners had been chartered to transport some of these antiques from Europe. Many were still in their packing cases, gathering the dust in the silent warehouses. They had never been opened, their contents never seen by Mr. Hearst, who had simply read a catalogue of a sale in Europe, and had cabled agents to purchase.

Antique lovers lined the way, and antique dealers lined their foreheads, trying to figure out how to keep prices up, once they had gone down at Gimbel's. Never, even in the apple-selling

days of the thirties, had they conjured up such a fearful fizzle.
What the particular dealer thought who had sold Mr. Hearst as
much as seven or eight million dollars' worth of antiquities is
unfortunately not on record.

The "laying out" took place in what had been the toy department on Gimbel's fifth floor, which looked, according to Edward
Alden Jewell, art critic of the *New York Times,* "as it never
looked before and as we may venture to guess it will never look
again." The gargantuan sale opened on February 3, 1941, and,
if the wisecrack made at the time that "Gimbel's cleared the
antique market at juicy savings," was not Gimbel's way of put-
ting it, the effect on public consciousness was just about that.

Life showed candid-camera shots of women bargain-hunters
among suits of armor. Peter Arno's cartoon in the *New Yorker,*
with the caption, "If you're so hell bent on buying something
that belongs to Mr. Hearst, you can get a *Journal American* for
three cents," was a note of hilarity unknown at any previous
antique auctions, and must have jarred the already frayed nerves
of the antique dealers.

"Besides the catalogue," wrote Mr. Jewell, "there are the
myriad white price tags. As for the price range, that in itself is
not the least extraordinary feature of an unexampled art world
event—thirty-five cents for little carved cats 'from the tomb of
Cleopatra' on up and up into the five and six figure bracket."

There were fireplaces from rooms used by Queen Elizabeth,
a Lady Hamilton bedroom, a portrait of Queen Henrietta Maria,
as well as the leavings of Cleopatra, and other celebrities of the
past. One wonders now why Gimbel's didn't go the whole hog
at the time and have the current Queen of Society knock them
down as auctioneer.

Furniture, in the dreary formations of a salesroom, looks hang-

dog enough even at best, but the effect of viewing Gimbel's fifth
floor on that far-off February morning must have been shatter-
ing. "Make no mistake," said Mr. Jewell, ". . . to stroll through
this prodigious commixion is an engrossing experience, even
though it entail an accompaniment of museum fatigue and department store feet."

What was overwhelming, was the appalling exposé of the
taste of a generation of rich men; and on top of this, the even
more surprising revelation of the bad taste of the various periods
to which the furniture and objects originally belonged. If historical romanticism and Victorian longings had blinded the generation of men who bought and sold this type of merchandise—
works of art—call it what you will—it did not appear in this light
to the kibitzing multitudes at Gimbel's. On they went, peering
and bargain-hunting among the remains of a monastery, a castle,
three French cloisters, panelled rooms, coffered ceilings, Aus-
trian chandeliers made of antlers, Dutch tiles, altar pieces, bed-
warmers, suits of armor, stained glass, and nineteenth-century
story-telling pictures, including one by Bouguereau, whose
"Nymphs and Satyr" was hung in the Hoffman House bar in
the eighties.

Though the crowds may not have realized it, they were seeing
at one and the same time, a retrospective exhibition and the end
of the era it portrayed. In the nation-wide attention which the
sale attracted, Americans could look back at the naïveté of an
older generation and see its mistaken longings to emulate old
Europe's mania for elaboration.

There were other signs that this taste of an older generation
was passing—the antique dealers themselves were thinning out.
Lord Duveen of Milbank and Charles Duveen were dead. Sir
Charles Allom had closed his shop. And along the stem of Fifth

Avenue, the châteaux and palazzos were disappearing like leaves from a tree.

Two years after the Hearst sale, another collection came under the hammer, this time at the Parke-Bernet Galleries—a sale as significant in its way as the Hearst sale. Mr. Condé Nast's collection, formerly in his apartment on Park Avenue, was offered at auction.

Mr. Nast's apartment had been filled with antique French furniture, backgrounds, and objets d'art, largely assembled for him by Elsie de Wolfe. In the preface of the sale catalogue, Elsie de Wolfe, now Lady Mendl, makes the astounding statement that "Mr. Nast's collection is . . . well adapted for small houses and the type of rooms in which most of us will, in the future, have to live." Even in 1943, she still clung to her dreams of America as one vast land of Trianon Villas.

Frank Crowninshield, the noted art critic, in this same preface, says: "Indeed, it has been freely remarked that millions of women, in America, England, and France, derived their principal ideas concerning desirable standards of living from Condé Nast." This is, of course, an allusion to the promotion of Condé Nast's tastes through his publications, notably *Vogue* and *House and Garden*. And the photographs which illustrate the catalogue very clearly show that Mr. Nast's "standards of living"—at least in decoration and furniture—which had been injected into the thinking of millions of women throughout the world, were really those of Elsie de Wolfe.

The sale was well publicized and well attended—a percentage of the audience being made up of European refugees; but the presence of Lady Mendl dominated. Sitting well to the front, she attested to her unchanging taste by doing considerable bidding on much of her former merchandise. It was thirty years since her book *The House in Good Taste* had been published, but her convictions were apparently unchanged. She remained the embodiment of the thinking and the taste of her generation.

The bidding was disappointingly low. Once again, as at the Hearst sale, the handwriting was on the wall, and not all the alleged glamor of Mr. Condé Nast and Lady Mendl combined could recreate the aura they had once thrown around the décor of a feudal France. If at the Hearst sale, the onlooker could observe the end of the fashion for Gothic and Renaissance, it seemed in the Parke-Bernet Galleries that the end of another fashion was also close at hand—that of antique French furniture which began with whistling bullfinches thirty-odd years before.

One month after the Condé Nast sale, there was another item of news that might well be observed by those who failed to take warning that the "days of plush and fanfare were numbered." This snippet was the announcement by the Lord & Taylor department store that they were throwing open to the public a "Going, Going, Gone Shop," where mirrors, antique furniture, objets d'art, and accessories get marked down until they sell.

The débâcle that began on the fifth floor of Gimbel's with the Hearst sale was indeed gathering impetus on the eighth floor of Lord & Taylor's; and the gloomy Nostradamus of the antique dealers, who warned that the inevitable end would come in Macy's basement, might well be a better prophet than he thought.

If this finale were to be postponed at all, the last hope lay in the coming of the European refugees, whose purchases were notable at the Condé Nast sale. This is no place for a dissertation on the vagaries of these fugitives, except in so far as they touch the antique picture. It would seem that life in America is made more tolerable for many of these Old World visitors if it can be lived in domestic surroundings that approximate closely those from which they were so unfortunately evicted by the latest change of conquerors. This is quite natural, and it should only be noted as an explanation of the flurry of new antique shops in New York, and the babel of unspoiled accents at the auction rooms. Let us hope it is only a temporary turning back of the clock, and come happier days, when Europe has reshuffled again, perhaps we may witness the unprecedented spectacle of antiques going from west to east across the Atlantic—a reversal of proceedings that would be an ironic footnote to the history of decorative art.

It is rumored over the antique back fences that one refugee of great wealth is buying all the old French furniture that is available, and filling a warehouse in New York in preparation for immediate shipment to Europe after the war, where he confidently believes such furniture will be at a premium. It is to be hoped not only for the future of America, but for the post-war homeland of this romantic antique merchant, that this gamble on Europe's pre-war love of the past is only a shot in the dark.

9. BAUHAUS BLUES

"All serves our New World progress, even the bafflers, head winds, cross tides. Through many perturbations and squalls and much backing and filling, the ship upon the whole makes unmistakably for her destination."

WALT WHITMAN

FROM the time that antique furniture and antique architecture throttled the daylights out of American houses, four attempts have been made to break the stranglehold. One of these attempts was American—the other three were European.

The first try came in 1900; it became world famous at the Exposition Universelle in Paris, where its success was rivalled only by Mistinguette in the Apache Dance, and the illumination on the Eiffel Tower. It was called Art Nouveau, and in the next ten years, it encrusted houses and furniture with its screwy fungoid shapes and barnacles.

Art Nouveau started in Belgium, which was the only country in Europe at the end of the nineteenth century to give a hand to those creative artists who were ignored because they were not in the tradition specified by the upper crust. Cézanne, Van Gogh, and Rodin were invited to Brussels, where a sympathetic and open-minded audience welcomed them; and in this audience was Henri van de Velde, whose particular dream baby was Art Nouveau.

This new style spread way beyond architecture, and affected furniture, jewelry, fabrics and typography, as well as inspiring, at a much later date, the ectoplasmic forms of Salvador Dali and the surrealist coterie. If you can imagine a bastard version of Louis XV furniture, decorated with carved escarole lettuce and *cuivre doré* tomatoes, in a room so overheated that the whole thing starts to melt into long running drips, you are visualizing Art Nouveau. There used to be a machine in candy shops that had

[71]

revolving metal arms which mixed a pale brown goo. As this sticky mess was drawn up, it undulated into the kind of shapes that were pure Henri van de Velde. Now do you get it?

The Germans were mad for Art Nouveau, or the Jugendstil, as it was called, just as they were mad for the Bauhaus which followed it there. In France, its great exponent was René Lalique, whose heavy iridescent glassware is still to be found standing on the folds of Spanish shawls on the grand pianos of grand opera singers all over the world. In America, the high priest of the movement was Louis Comfort Tiffany, who, after decorating the homes of America with much stained glass and mosaic, had the birthday of his life in Mexico City. Here in the opera house, he created a gigantic fire curtain of colored glass cubes, designed to appear as "a vast window intersected by square mullions, beyond which a magical landscape unfolds itself." A colossal lump of luxury which, by the way, is still hoisted up and down to gasps of wonderment, and has to be seen to be credited.

The last traces of Art Nouveau have supposedly disappeared completely now, but it pops up here and there, as it did in Metro-Goldwyn's *Marie Antoinette*, when Norma Shearer picked up what was supposed to be a Louis XVI hand mirror, but what was in reality a scrap of Art Nouveau straight from some Trianon shoppe at Hollywood Boulevard and Vine. And if this brings the pink to the cheeks of Cedric Gibbons as well as Louis B., it's becoming to them anyway.

In addition to Miss Shearer's hand mirror, most of the jewelry (with the possible exception of Verdura's) that is smirking in the Fifth Avenue emporiums at this minute, is pure Art Nouveau, and a blood relation of the cast iron bridges in Central Park.

Art Nouveau was as gooey as a twenty-five cent valentine. Compared with the roast beef of English antiques and the *pomme soufflé* of the French ones, it probably had the effect of a strawberry parfait. But it was at least the beginning of a struggle in Europe to break the imperious control of the taste of the old rich and of the *nouveaux riches* who truckled to it.

Art Nouveau was a brave and brief struggle against the octopus of tradition, but since its originators thought of their innovation entirely in terms of applied decoration, it remained only a short-lived fashion. Baffled and passé, it passed out. The effort had failed, and the power of the antique dealers and period architects was greater than before. So much for the first attempt to break the stranglehold.

The second try was American, and it came about 1910. It was called, rather unfortunately, the "Mission style," but it is important because it was an attempt to develop furniture which for all its Spanish origins, had acquired some American characteristics in California.

"Mission furniture," says the Grand Rapids Furniture Recorder of that day, "is really a type rather than a style. Its origin, as the name would imply, is in the early Spanish California missions of the Jesuits. An old chair and settee from an ancient mission house, secured by a collector of odd and antique furniture, furnished the inspiration of the style."

The effect of this furniture on a fashionable Brooklyn decorator is also recorded for posterity. Brooklynites, by the way, were as Paris-minded in 1910 as Fifth Avenue, and the *Brooklyn Daily Eagle* ran a whole page called "The News and Views of Paris."

People "will have Mission furniture this season," says the aforementioned decorator, "even if they mix it with Colonial tables and Chippendale chairs in a room with Empire decorations, the carpet of Louis XVI design. That is one of the annoying things that we decorators and furnishers have to contend with.

"Now we decorated a handsome new house this spring, each room in a distinctive style and calling for furnishings to match. But the owners finally concluded to select the furnishings themselves and filled the house with a lot of promiscuous stuff bought haphazard here and there. I happened to look in at the finished state and received a nervous shock at the sight.

"I do not know," he goes on, quivering from this exposure, "how long the Mission will hold sway, but I am willing to bet that the Colonial styles will continue to the end of time."

In this snobbish hysteria, we can see the Mission didn't stand a chance. Brooklyn ladies saw themselves like Miss Shearer as Marie Antoinette—not as Jesuit fathers. The most flattering expression of the time was "fit for a queen," and it was unlikely that "fit for a Jesuit missionary" would be equally flattering. There would be no inducement to giving a lap supper or some *tableaux vivants* in the atmosphere of a mission—California or otherwise.

When the Metropolitan Museum of Art opened the American Wing in 1924, dedicated to the Colonial style, Brooklyn knew it had been right all along; another *crise de nerfs* had been weathered by the fashionable decorators. The second slug at antiques was a flop, and, as Emily Post had it, "sweet, ordinary, every-day, semi-Colonial, semi-French and semi-Italian" were the order of the day.

In 1925, Paris launched something called "Modern," which was an attempt to create the richness and elaboration of period French rooms, without using any period designs to do it. The results of this effort produced the Radio City Music Hall. It also produced the interiors of the *Normandie*, a large part of the

Waldorf Astoria, the lounge cars on the Super Chief, and one hell of a temper in Mrs. Emily Post, who liked her French *semi* or not at all.

Department stores and gift shops fell for the "Modern," with its stylized flower-pattern carpets, colored mirrors, zebra skins, fur-covered chairs, and stepped-up bookcases. There was quite a flurry for a time. But time was on the side of the antiquarians, it seemed, and Modern, after a lingering death in night clubs, finally joined the Mission in the limbo of the unfashionable.

The third attempt had come and gone.

Meanwhile, back in Europe our old friend Henri van de Velde, famous for his Art Nouveau, had a terrific break. He was invited to Weimar by the Grand Duke of Sachsen-Weimar. The Grand Duke, bless his heart, was a patron of the arts, and Weimar the center of "classic German culture." Henri and the Duke became buddies, and Henri became one of the leaders in this cultural hideaway, and founded what became the Bauhaus.

The Bauhaus was a school of design, or if you prefer it, a laboratory of design. Architecture and furniture were included, together with all forms of creative work. The dream of the founders was that architecture, sculpture, and painting would be completely integrated in the buildings of the future, which was pretty sound thinking, it seems to me.

Shortly after the great exhibition of the Bauhaus in 1923, Americans began to get interested, just as they had been interested in Art Nouveau after the Exhibition in Paris in 1900. Although the founder of both these movements was the same man, the Bauhaus was not (God forbid) Art Nouveau. In 1933, the Bauhaus closed its doors, Hitler preferring his own architecture, but its history and its accomplishments were revealed five years later in America at an exhibition held at the Museum of Modern Art in New York. Thus the Bauhaus was the fourth attempt to interest Americans in contemporary European designs instead of dead historical ones.

And that brings us up almost to this minute. What effect the Bauhaus will have—what its contribution to architecture in America will be—remains to be seen.

Some of its most distinguished ex-members are now in America, and building houses here. The most famous of these are Walter Gropius and Marcel Breuer.

"These two men," said *Fortune,* in January 1942, "are best known for their work at the Bauhaus in Germany, where they helped develop the coldly intellectual 'international style' in modern architecture."

This "international style" has other elements in it besides the Bauhaus—the Finnish element, identified by the buildings and furniture of Alvar Aalto; and the French element, which is summed up in the work of Le Corbusier.

The most famous innovation of the Bauhaus is the tubular steel furniture, since manufactured all over the world, and particularly noticeable today in American cafeterias and drug stores.

The furniture of Alvar Aalto is the descendant of the perforated curved plywood used for railroad and ferry seating, which was invented by Americans in the 1870's. Alvar Aalto carries this early curved plywood design a stage further by giving it a wood-supporting frame, and it is for this type of furniture that he is famous. The effect is that of a seat and back, sometimes upholstered, suspended between a pair of skiis bent to beautiful and graceful lines.

Le Corbusier, primarily an architect, is perhaps best known to the American public as the man who gave houses the definition that they are "machines for living." His architecture is much admired in Latin America, and while the United States has no examples, the influence of Le Corbusier was strikingly obvious in the better sections of the New York World's Fair.

Whether all this combines to create an international style which is coldly intellectual, as opposed to antique styles which are, let us say, "feverishly imbecile," is something one need not get into too many arguments about. More important than the international style and the antique style is the indigenous American architecture, which quietly came about long before such argument even began.

But before considering this great movement, suppose we trace the history of furniture design—so lean forward in your jury box and review the case.

10. CHARGE TO THE JURY

"A new world, a new chance, with oceans to wall in the new thought against interference from the old! . . .

"O Eagle! . . . Thou wert to be the advance-guard of humanity, the herald of all progress; how often hast thou betrayed this high commission! . . ."

MARGARET FULLER

IN THE entire history of furniture, beginning thousands of years ago, furniture was designed and made to order. It was always bought as new furniture, and from the time of the Pharaohs until the nineteenth century it came directly from the cabinetmaker's bench to the palace, or castle, or house for which it had been ordered.

Each generation evolved a style from the preceding one, and made this new style expressive of its own taste and time.

In the beginning, this evolution was slow. In Greece during the fourth and fifth centuries B.C.—the meridian of Western art—the furniture designers, like the architects, confined themselves to a few generic types, and devoted their energies to developing and perfecting these, rather than inventing new designs. The Greek chair called the klismos, perhaps the most beautiful chair ever made in the world, was a design in use for at least three hundred years.

In the ages which follow the Greek democracy, this custom of slowly perfecting basic models begins to disappear, and there is an ever-quickening desire to change designs, not with the idea of improving them, but simply to follow the whims of the ruling class, or the fashionable.

This fashionable motivation produced only elaboration and eccentricity, a fact which is clearly verified by comparing the furniture made in France and England during the two hundred

[79]

years from 1610 to 1810 with the furniture of Greece in the fourth and fifth centuries B.C.

In France during this period, there were *eight* distinctly recognizable changes of styles, and in England during this same time, there were *ten* distinct styles—producing only elaboration in cabinetmaking and ornamentation, without any real improvement in design. In Greece during the fourth and fifth centuries B.C., there is no radical change in style—only a constant perfecting of a basic type, with the resultant simplicity and beauty.

With the coming of the Industrial Revolution in the nineteenth century there appears a large group of industrial millionaires who, for the first time in the history of the world, buy the furniture of the older aristocracy in order to emulate them and become identified with them.

The fashion of using antique furniture was originated by these *nouveaux riches* of the nineteenth century. *It is essentially a nouveau-riche idea*, an historical fact that has been carefully overlooked and avoided by the antique dealers and interior decorators of the world.

The aristocracy which originally owned this now antique furniture had had it made for them, and when they received it in their homes, it was brand new contemporary furniture. They liked new furniture of their own period, and would have thought it absurd to buy anything made for people of a previous period—as absurd as we would think it today to go out and buy an old ice box instead of a new refrigerator, especially if the old ice box cost more than the new model.

The idea of buying antique furniture spread from the *nouveaux riches* of Europe to the middle classes, and when the new millionaires of America arrived in Europe, they found antique furniture buying an established part of the social life they had determined to emulate. These American *nouveaux riches* brought back the antique fashion to America, where it was spread through the entire country by the ignorance, snobbery, and commercial instincts of the early architects, interior decorators, magazines, and, finally, Grand Rapids.

As a result of this combination, which induced mass acceptance of the antique fashion, American houses and furniture have failed to become a part of the American democratic individuality. At least fifty years of the life of American architecture and furniture have been thrown away—fifty wasted years of confusion and futility, during which time America could have raised furniture design and architecture to the high levels of its other achievements.

Today we stand confronted with the piled-up debris resulting from this folly and madness. It is all around us, deadening our lives, choking the storage warehouses, and streaming through the auction galleries—the dead refuse of the dead from the lumber rooms of the old world.

American houses have become the rubbish dumps of Europe, and the maudlin, morbid preoccupation with the decaying refuse of the past, a part of American thinking.

It is an ironic commentary on a proud people, who slashed the umbilical cord which tied them to a feudal past, that they should end with an inferiority complex about the actual material manifestations of this same feudalism, and set their furniture industries to imitating it with hundreds of thousands of bastardized copies.

"The sere remains of foreign harvests" have been garnered to the last mildewed stalk, and the American barn, to be frank, is filled with as much decaying fodder as it will hold.

Three attempts to import European styles, which were a revolt against their own historical junk, have come; and two have definitely gone.

Experts estimate that America needs at least nine hundred thousand new houses every year for ten years after the war. America stands facing this vast future of the post-war world with a furniture industry which is obsolete, and a public which is punch-drunk from antique decorating.

Unless by a miracle the thinking of America changes, this post-war flood of housing might mean an even greater swarming of the locusts of antiquity; and plane flights from coast to coast will be made over the roof-tops of Cape Cod, Queen Anne, Georgian and Colonial settlements, with a strong dose of Hollywood Chippendale waiting at the California end.

This persistent ghost-walking is already haunting the thinking of many Americans, not all of whom are architects. Indeed, there are men who were haunted long ago by the horrors which are all around us now, and which they were powerless to prevent, though they devoted their lives to a vain struggle to forestall the debacle.

Some of these men, and some of the thinking about post-war American houses, you will find in the next chapter, after turning the asbestos fire curtain which separates them from the preceding records of futility and *chi-chi*. That was the most I could do to spare their obvious embarrassment at finding themselves at such a weird historical cocktail party.

You will now proceed and find your verdict.

11. THIS IS WHERE YOU CAME IN

"By 1932 a cloud of dust blew from the new wheat lands, obscuring the sun in Washington and filtering through the windows of houses in Arizona and Texas. Meantime, great dams began to be built. A veil of green, reclaimed land spread over tens of thousands of acres that had been desert for centuries. Green crept again over the dust bowl. The land wounded by erosion began to heal. Cover crops moored down the soil again with a web of interlocking roots.

"On the farms themselves, from the Tennessee Valley throughout the country, electric lights glimmered where there had been no lights before. Tasks of all sorts were being performed by electric power. Machines demanded larger farms. Farms of more than 500 acres increased 37% in the decade from 1930 to 1940. The immemorial way of the farmer had altered."

MARY HEATON VORSE

On an evening in May, 1939, the great hall of the Royal Institute of British Architects in London was jammed with an audience that overflowed into the aisles and lined the walls. The atmosphere, we are told, "was charged with a strange expectancy. No architectural speaker in London had ever in living memory gathered such an audience."

The event that had galvanized the ponderous superiority of British architects to this point of "strange expectancy," was something unprecedented in their entire history. The lecturer they had come to hear was an American whose work and philosophy had challenged all the previous architectural thinking of the world. It was Frank Lloyd Wright.

In the jittery pre-war Europe of 1939, the presence of Frank Lloyd Wright was more than an omen that the day had already come when Europe would look to America for its architectural inspiration, instead of to antique Italy and Greece—an idea which should give many an American millionaire and many an antique dealer goose pimples, as well as pause to think.

[83]

"Life has not yet gone very far forward with us," Wright told his stunned audience, "when we are still back with the Franco-Georgian tradition, and with these great old Renaissance palaces you treasure.

"Again I ask where did you get them? Ask yourselves where they came from to you in England. I know, as every architect who thinks must know, that buildings of that insane period are no longer treasures, that they were a mere mask upon a meretricious life and are in no sense revealing or evolutionary where modern life is concerned except as a horrible example. We know, if we care to know, that they lack integrity in every sense."

For four evenings the white-haired American missionary of architecture talked on and on to this audience which had sent across the Atlantic for him. At the end of the second evening, a weariness came over him. Perhaps he had looked again at London and at England, and sensed the pre-war despondency and impotence in high places, the crushing weight of old age and tradition in those who controlled architecture, and the sword of Damocles hanging over all the exhaustion and stubbornness.

"Now I have talked enough. Really talking is of very little value, I feel. I am always ashamed to be doing it publicly but . . . still . . . I do it. After I have given a talk of this kind I go home depressed thinking to myself: 'Here I am at it again trying, trying, trying, and what is the use?' "

It was true. He had been talking and trying for more than fifty years, and that's a long way back on anyone's passport. No wonder, as he looked around at this new and troubled generation, a momentary depression overtook him.

It was forty-three years since he had spoken at the University Guild, Evanston, Illinois. He was a young man of twenty-six then, but the message was the same—always the same: "The fashions and fads of our typical street grit the teeth of one so foolish as to take the matter seriously. Colonial and Renaissance, the château and the chalet. Anything that one can feel quite sure happened sometime, somewhere, and was not ridiculous; anything that is not our own; anything that is not American."

In 1900 when the Vanderbilts were launched in their Gothic château, and Fifth Avenue was buying Beaux Arts, he said: "It was my ill fortune to be shown through the palace of one of Chicago's great captains of industry. . . . There was no single beautiful touch to mitigate the horrors of the 'tout ensemble.' . . . Such homes are the result of a lust for possession . . . and this lust is as conspicuous in the homes of New York's Four Hundred as in the homes of their more clumsy Chicago imitators. Such perversion is contaminating to a degree we dimly realize, and concerns us all."

No wonder he was depressed as he walked the streets of London on those May evenings in 1939. As a boy he had seen the remnants of American Gothic replaced by the fresh horrors of the imaginings of Sir Charles Eastlake. He had watched the Turkish corner come and go, and the Chicago Fair, and the Beaux Arts, and Elsie de Wolfe. He had watched Americans like drunken sailors buying French Gothic, English Tudor, French Louis, Italian, Spanish, Victorian, and Swedish from the antique markets of Europe. Then he had looked again at the old world, filled with antique shops and antique architecture, new and old. "I go home depressed thinking to myself: 'Here I am at it again, trying, trying, trying, and what is the use?'"

Other men besides Frank Lloyd Wright had watched this cavalcade of foreign importations while they struggled to give democracy its birthright in architecture. The record of their struggle is the history of the architecture which we now know as American.

Perhaps one of the greatest of these men was Louis Sullivan, who died in 1924. He died comparatively poor, and very lonely. His office was gone, his library auctioned off, and his home was a small hotel room in Chicago.

"They killed Sullivan, and they nearly killed me," said Frank Lloyd Wright, to whom Sullivan was "Lieber Meister" since the day in 1887 when they met—a fortunate day for America, by the way, for much of the teaching of "Lieber Meister" went into making Wright its greatest architect.

Chicago in the nineties was quite a place, and something was happening there that America was unaware of at the time. Business was good (it knew that of course), and Chicago's population was rising (which it also knew), but it failed to see that a group of men was creating buildings to accommodate this new tide of business—buildings that were as new in conception as were the democratic ideas of the people they housed.

In the First Leiter building, the Manhattan, Marquette and Reliance buildings, and the Carson Pirie Scott department store, for the first time in the world, engineer and architect collaborated and produced new forms in which construction and architecture became indissoluble. These Chicago buildings were the beginning of the modern business buildings of the world; with their creation, architecture took on a new and splendid lease for its future life.

The attitude of mind of the men responsible for this is explained very simply for us by Louis Sullivan in an address he made to the Chicago Architectural Club on May 30, 1899. Read what he said, and read it carefully, because in it you will discover American architecture's declaration of independence.

"I urge that you cast away as worthless the shop-worn and empirical notion that an architect is an artist—and accept my assurance that he is and imperatively shall be an interpreter of the national life of his time. . . . You are called upon, not to betray, but to express the life of your own day and generation. . . . A fraudulent and surreptitious use of historical documents, however suavely presented, however cleverly plagiarized, however neatly repacked, however shrewdly intrigued, will constitute and will be held to be a betrayal of trust. . . . If you take the pains truly to understand your country, your people, your day, your generation; the time, the place in which you live . . . you will be understood and sympathetically received in return."

The fact that twenty-five years later Sullivan, alone and dying, knew that he had not really been understood, nor sympathetically received, only gives emphasis to the newness of his thinking and the incomprehension of his contemporaries.

But the torch was in good fighting hands. "New York still believes," said Frank Lloyd Wright, "that art should be imported; brought over in ships; and is a quite contented market place. . . .

"Louis Sullivan gave America the skyscraper as an organic modern work of art. While America's architects were stumbling at its height, piling one thing on top of another, foolishly denying it, Louis Sullivan seized its height as its characteristic feature, and made it sing; a new thing under the sun! One of the world's greatest architects, he gave us again the ideal of a great architecture that informed all the great architectures of the world."

In 1910, while America pottered amongst its Chippendale and pseudo-palace memorabilia, a German exchange professor, Kuno Francke, was responsible for making Frank Lloyd Wright internationally famous long before America became aware of his presence. In Germany he published a monumental work on Wright's architecture.

In 1915, while Mr. Henry Frick sent Elsie de Wolfe to Paris to buy antiques at ten per cent commission, and the rest of America sent for its annual shipments of antiques (it spent $18,475,000 for them that particular year), the Japanese sent a Commission around the world to select an architect for the Imperial Hotel in Tokyo.

The hotel, which was to be a modern building, had to be designed to outwit the earthquakes which were forever shuddering under and around the busy little island.

The Commission, after deliberating the talents of the architectural world, decided that in Frank Lloyd Wright it had found a great architect, and the only man who could possibly undertake this outright defiance of the menace of nature.

Their judgment amounted to clairvoyance. Seven years later, balancing on its concrete piers like a tray on a waiter's fingers, the architectural masterpiece was completed. "Banzai, Wrieto-San, Banzai," yelled his sixty foremen from the docks of Yokohama, as Wright sailed down the bay.

Two years later, in 1924, the earthquake struck, convulsing Tokyo and Yokohama into wastes of flaming rubble, and the Imperial Hotel was reported to have crumbled with the rest.

After ten days of rumor and uncertainty, Wright received a telegram from Baron Okura: "IMPERIAL STANDS UNDAMAGED A MONUMENT TO YOUR GENIUS IN JAPAN THOUSANDS OF HOMELESS PROVIDED WITH UNINTERRUPTED SERVICE CONGRATULATIONS."

America now sat up and took notice, but it had taken an earthquake to do it. No! I'm wrong. Not all the country sat up because of all the houses that Wright built following this period, not one was in Boston or New York.

"The regeneration of architecture," said Wright, "does not lie in the hands of classicists or fashion-mongers of the East nor of the West. Their work is almost written at its length, and no spark of life and but a shroud of artistic respectability will cling to it half a century hence.

"It is but archaeological dry bones bleaching in the sun."

Frank Lloyd Wright is now over seventy, and a generation of young architects, inspired by his example, is at work. Their houses are on the hills of California, the plains of the Middle West, and the deserts of Arizona, some worthy of the master, some not; but all belonging, because of his teaching, to the soil of America.

It has been said of Frank Lloyd Wright that his work bestrides the entire epoch, and his influence has colored the architectural thinking of at least two generations in America and Europe. It might also be added that it was Wright who challenged and scattered the dead ghosts of the old world that haunted American architecture and opened the way to its complete identification with the needs and expressions of democracy.

These houses have a new spaciousness extending beyond the limits of the walls, through wide windows that link the lives of the inhabitants with the life of nature surrounding them. Gone are the old box-like rooms, with their dense shut-in atmosphere and congested furnishing. The menacing claustrophobia of period houses, which drove families out to porches, golf clubs, and automobile escapism, has been banished, and a sense of peace and open air pervades the new interiors in which so much of their life is spent.

Instead of the lugubrious sighing for the past that surrounds antique furniture, a fresh, cheerful awareness of the present seems to envelop these new houses. For the first time in history, the security that man is striving for is expressed in the way he lives. Gone are the last traces of battlements and moats, encircling walls, the hiding from feudal poverty in vast secluded acreage, shuttered windows, and bedrooms beyond the reach of night raids by Indians.

"Any building which is built should love the ground on which it stands," said Wright. One cannot do better than to let it go at that. Above all else, the houses of Wright and his younger followers are united completely with the contours of the land on which they stand so proudly.

If the Chicago school of architecture in the nineties was the opening gambit of American architecture, the second phase came fifty years later. The scene of its inauguration is the Tennessee River in 1933, where the Tennessee Valley Authority, or TVA as it is better known, began work on splitting the river into a chain of lakes seven hundred miles long.

To accomplish this, as well as to control the watershed, a network of twenty-eight great dams was put into construction or operation. The roar of the blasting and the grinding of giant power shovels heaving the upturned muck, together with the other muckraking noises from the TVA political battleground at Washington, are dying away, and we can now review quietly the architectural accomplishments and significance of this stupendous project.

In the great valley a new architecture is seen in vigorous action. It is the architecture of public welfare—the architecture of utilitarianism—the ultimate architecture of democracy. Completely and finally emancipated from previous architectural dogma, these superb creations are America's answer and challenge to the embalmed survivance of the past, as well as to the more recent megalithic monstrosities of Fascism.

The union of architecture and engineering, and the search for purity of form, which had begun with the Chicago architects of the nineties, arrives at a splendid coming of age in these great masterpieces of the Tennessee Valley. In the towering bastions of concrete, the powerhouses sheltering the gleaming turbines, in the laboratories, the switch yards, and the pylons carrying the high-tension wires to remote cities and farms is a new architectural order of extraordinary beauty and precision— the first reality of a future that might be brighter than the lamps the dams have already lighted, and more fruitful than the land that they have reclaimed for future generations.

In the Tennessee Valley America has shown that a *people's* architecture can also be reckoned among the great architecture of the world, and that the age of mechanical power has an inherent aesthetic force of dazzling potency undreamed of by previous ages. Already this great project has become a mecca for architects, engineering experts, and technical groups from Great Britain, South America, China and Russia, faced with similar twentieth-century problems, and eager to learn from America's solution of them.

With this vast accomplishment in mind, we can see, as we review briefly the work to be done, the pattern that the future architecture of America will follow.

According to the Department of Agriculture, between two and three million farmhouses are needed today in the United States. Thousands of the existing farmhouses are "below the standard, not only of the twentieth century, but the nineteenth or eighteenth century. . . . They are not only far below our American standards of living, they are even worse than the houses of many Chinese peasants." This fearful chaos has come about while America has wasted time, money, and energy for the last fifty years wistfully recalling the architecture and furniture of Europe. This is a slap in the face of a democracy which has been thoughtless, and it would be well to bear it in mind when plans are made for housing this same democracy in a post-war world. After the war, millions of people will have to be rehoused. In defense housing, there is evidence that American architects of the present generation are prepared for the test. But we cannot be equally optimistic about the furniture for these post-war houses.

I remarked at the beginning of this book that when it came to the moment for furnishing thousands of defense houses, it was discovered that there was practically no contemporary American furniture being manufactured that was suitable to use in them. This very grim and alarming revelation is, of course, the direct result of America's shindig of antique worship.

The Grand Rapids commercial manufacturer mentality is a completely obsolete mentality. Why shouldn't it be? It is at one with the equally obsolete thinking of antique punch-drunk interior decoration magazines, interior decorators, and department store buyers. From the day in 1848 when the first circular saw and lathe were installed in Grand Rapids, Michigan, it is impossible to detect in the entire record one sign of artistry, or one sign of any effort to establish a really contemporary American style. The complete history is one of downright pandering to any God-forsaken idea that filtered through from antique furniture history books, decorators, buyers or magazines.

Not a single piece of furniture has come out of this hotbed of vulgarity, sterility and ignorance that would indicate that its so-called designers have seen anything in the contemporary architecture of America as an inspiration for new and fresh furniture. They have made no effort to replace the dowdy caricatures and reproductions of antiques which have always formed their major market.

From the days of Gothic brass beds, Queen Anne parlor suites, and Louis XIV quartered oak chiffoniers, down to the bastard concoctions of today, designated by such dubious labels as "French Provincial Modern," "Classic Modern," etc., the commercial furniture groups have foisted off on the American public the most frightful grab-bag of deformity, garishness, and pretentiousness ever put together in the entire history of human habitation.

It would seem incredible that this could continue indefinitely, and yet, beyond a feeble effort here and there in the group, there is nothing to indicate that the good contemporary American furniture needed right now, and more so after the war, is anywhere in sight.

At this moment, much of the time and effort of the furniture industry is taken up making aeroplane parts and gliders, mostly of molded plywood; and it is perhaps possible that this new experience and contact with the more vital contemporary-minded aeroplane-manufacturing personalities may bring the light of day to Grand Rapids. It *is* possible, but such thinking must be regarded cautiously.

Perhaps the prefabricated house will do away with Grand Rapids. There's a thought to put under your pillow together with the crumbs of the wedding cake—prefabricated Grand Rapidless houses, and happiness ever after!

There has been a lot of bright and not-so-bright chatter, to say nothing of a prediction or two, about these theoretical houses of the future. Thurman Arnold, the former Yale professor, for instance, has been doing a little prefabricated house crystal gazing between trust-busting. And this is what he saw, as the clouds in the post-war daydream cleared away:

"Every man can have a new house prefabricated out of magnesium for two thousand dollars and he will need a double aluminum garage in which to park his two cars, which Henry Ford will be stamping out of soybeans. . . ." This soothsaying was followed by a little tea-leaf reading by Henry Kaiser, who promised America a prefabricated six-room house, demountable, completely furnished, insulated, and equipped with all sanitary and disposal facilities for fifteen hundred dollars.

These salmon-pink prognostications are all a part of the type of thinking which came from Jules Verne via H. G. Wells, via Norman Bel Geddes, via Superman, to today. And now, with post-war speculation rampant, everyone wants to get a crack at it.

It is egged on by the scientists in particular, who react this way in wartime. Having let hell loose by producing everything possible for humanity to annihilate itself, they start swishing their test tubes again and promise to spawn up some Utopian materials which will turn the world into a laboratory-made Garden of Eden come peacetime. They are talking at the moment of silk made from coal, fire-resistant wood, bendable glass, two-way private radios, furniture derived from air, water, and coal, plastic automobiles, plastic houses, plastic-banded and plastic-impregnated plywood, and finally, of course, plastic coffins.

In contrast to this plethora of futuristic voodoo and speculation on soybean cars, magnesium houses, and the Futurama of the World's Fair, masterpieces of engineering and architecture, such as the Merritt Parkway, the Hutchinson River Parkway, the Triborough Bridge, to say nothing of the Tennessee Valley project, were already realities. Furthermore, the primary aim of prefabrication—to produce houses on a mass-production basis—is *not* new; it has existed since the nineteenth century.

Since the average yearly income is supposed to be about twenty-five hundred dollars for eighty-seven per cent of the population, it seems possible that a large percentage of the public may send for a "mail order" house costing two thousand dollars—presuming they cherish the idea of living in one of these houses, which one should not take for granted. But assuming that they do, by what miracle are we to expect that the mentality that is creating and manufacturing these houses will suddenly become superior to the mentality that has governed the commercial furniture manufacturers and the speculative builders for the last fifty years?

It is one thing for the Farm Security Administration, the Tennessee Valley Authority, and the Federal housing agencies, with their power of jurisdiction, their capable staffs, and their experience, to sponsor the development and planning of communities in which hundreds of prefabricated houses have been used more or less successfully. But what lies ahead when similar projects are undertaken by anyone who can afford to build a plant, turn out the houses, and sell them to any speculative builder who owns a building lot—to say nothing of thousands of individuals who might want to pop one into the first neck of the woods they happen to see? How are we to know that the prefabricated house will not be a worse evil than the billboard as far as eyesores go?

As to the plastic millennium which we are told by the chemists is at hand, I had a plastic drinking glass in my bathroom, and every time I rinsed my teeth, it felt like drinking out of the top of a thermos bottle at a picnic. I like picnics, but not in my own bathroom.

Every man can remember the time the chemists dreamed up shirt collars of celluloid, which eventually ended as my plastic glass did, in one hell of a fine blaze. I will say this for them—they're great for kindling.

Lately there has been a plastic concocted which looks like clear mint drops, and the furniture manufacturers have turned out some horrors made of it that look like a tart's dream of modernistic. If this is a foretaste of the caskets in which the post-war deceased will set forth to meet their Maker, there ought to be a fine post-war rush on cremation.

"Destined to become a popular tableware of the world of to-morrow," says the Office of War Information, "are the new improved plastic dishes now being used about United States naval vessels and patrol bombers. . . . They are used on all ships smaller than destroyers because the firing of the guns played havoc with the mess crockery in smaller vessels." Of the cups used on patrol bombers, the OWI says: "On the cups a deep cup-stand 'locks' the cup even to as sharp an angle as thirty degrees."

Now while I agree that housewives in Kalamazoo have better crockery coming to them in peacetime, I fail to see what a cup of alpha-cellulose filled melamine formaldehyde, shatter-proof under gunfire and dive-bombing, and thirty-degree tip-proof, has to do with a quiet dish of tea between rubbers in a post-war world.

No! I think plastics are all very well in their right places, and my idea of the right place is a vacuum cleaner nozzle, a refrigerator part, or a telephone. But the golden age of plastic wall coverings and furniture . . . God forbid !

The way the decorators, the magazines, and the furniture manufacturers feel about it right now, if you let them loose with

Chippendale in Plastic

prefabricated houses and plastics, the results would be magnesium Cape Cod cottages, Georgian villas, and French Provincial farmhouses rolling off the prefabricated assembly lines; while out of the plastic molds would come a stream of plastic cobblers' benches, Chippendale piecrust tables, and corner cupboards in the colors of the rainbow. And the way the public is being brought up right now, this chemical chow mein would be just its dish.

Just let me add this and then we can drop the subject. Plastics are wonderful. Prefabricated houses are wonderful. And the post-war world will be full of them if the big corporations get their plans through, which they usually do. But both innovations can and will add further aesthetic horror to our lives unless they are controlled and handled by better brains and better taste than those controlling similar innovations in the pre-war days.

America needs more than the dreams of a plastic millennium as seen by E. I. duPont de Nemours and Company, or prefabricated ends of the rainbow as seen by Thurman Arnold and others, if it is to produce better homes for its homeless post-war millions. And the sooner we promote some realistic thinking about this, the better the prospects will be of getting them.

The optimists who think that an architectural millennium will automatically occur after the war must have had more than a shock when they saw the Royal Academy version of post-blitz London. The millennium in this case turned out to be a rehash of the pompous paraphernalia of the nineteenth-century Paris Beaux Arts School of Architects, in which the London of the future appeared as one vast extension of Selfridge's department store. "Something like this," wrote Professor C. H. Reilly, the eminent English architect, "was only to be expected from this Academy group of architects. They have rejected each year from the architectural room in their Summer Exhibition any designs for buildings to which the words 'modern' or 'contemporary' could be applied, and that in spite of a world-wide movement extending over the last thirty years."

Concurrently with the exhibition of this regurgitated Georgiana, is a movement by the leading British architectural magazines to institute parliamentary action for the immediate demobilization of architects, builders and engineers after the war, so that reconstruction and planning can begin with the least delay. To give these younger people a chance, it might be wiser, in view of the debacle at the Royal Academy, to restrain the older generation *right now*, not only in Britain but in America as well, before it gets busy on further grave-digging sprees in the Beaux Arts cemetery and the Colonial catacombs.

As far as the interior of houses goes, the average American man has most of his thinking regarding this part of his life done for him by his wife and her sisterhood of the interior-decoration seraglio, of whom the kindest thing that can be said is that they have revealed, with glamorous femininity, ideas of unparalleled confusion.

It is from this source that the antiquarian heresy has been nurtured and propagandized through the magazines, until, via the Grand Rapids assembly lines, its mass sterility is foisted off on innocent millions throughout the country. These same millions are still at the mercy of this thinking, and so are their post-war homes, to say nothing of millions of their dollars, which will probably go to pay for more boatloads of post-war European junk pouring in duty free. Incidentally, if the billion dollars spent on antiques from 1910 to 1940 had gone towards a few good institutions for research on the needs of American houses, we would *have* good contemporary furniture *today*, and America would be prepared to undertake post-war reconstruction with greater resources than any country in the world.

The money and the time have gone but the bad thinking remains, only awaiting the end of the war to add more chaos to the existing accumulation.

The experience gained by the Farm Security Administration, the Tennessee Valley Authority and the U. S. Housing Authority, can be the basis of a large pool of knowledge that will undertake to re-educate the people of America towards better solutions—and contemporary American solutions—for their houses, and particularly for their furniture, since some form of supervised education must be undertaken other than that which prevailed in the past and is prevailing now.

The young generation that will begin its peacetime life in the future deserves something better than the sterile hash surrounding us now. These young Americans, with their wartime troubles over, should not be left at the mercy of the present system when they come to spend their savings on their first home. Their money should buy them something better than the monstrosities which are peddled in every furniture store and department store in thousands of large and small towns throughout the country.

Decent surroundings in the home at prices which all can afford are a vital national need. They are an important part of mental and physical well-being, and as such they deserve national concerted action—and the sooner the better.

The ills of American furniture are beyond quick recovery by means of a strong dose of plastics and prefabricated houses, as those in possession of the over-all picture know only too well. The antique furniture cancer is a deeply rooted evil, forever sapping the strength of healthy national and contemporary

thinking, and it must be cut away before any kind of future well-being in houses can be thought of or even hoped for.

If America can labor and bring forth the TVA, one need not despair because its furniture was a miscarriage—the next accouchement may produce a native son. One might begin to plant the seeds for this by training groups of furniture designers in architectural schools to work in close collaboration with contemporary architects, so that the new furniture dovetails accurately with the accomplished definitions of American architecture. In other words, side by side with the site planning, the engineering, and the architecture of future communities goes a simultaneous planning and production of appropriate furniture.

Work on organizing such a group of furniture designers should not be left to the end of the war. It is of the utmost urgency that it begin now, because it entails a vast experimentation and research on a national scale. Post-war American architecture, thanks to men like Louis Sullivan, Frank Lloyd Wright and their younger followers, has a good solid foundation on which to go forward after the war.

American furniture has no such foundation. American furniture is non-existent, and whoever starts out to materialize it starts from scratch—from absolute scratch. That is why the urgency is great, and why the job must be tackled now. The nucleus, at least, of such furniture must be ready soon, so that a study can begin for its mass production immediately after the war.

The furniture manufacturers are becoming absorbed in war work; the furniture now being made is from old models, which were sour long before they were frozen; and it is extremely questionable whether many of the present manufacturers will carry on any experiments for new post-war designs, even if their designers are capable of doing so.

The result of all this will mean that in order to meet the post-war demand, they will resurrect obsolete models and flood the market with them. And the public, impatient and unprepared for better things, will probably buy them as fast as they can be turned out.

There are thinking men in America who can forestall this if they act in time. And though the time is short and the work to be done overwhelming, it can be done, and its fulfillment will not be lightly dismissed by future historians recounting the stages by which America brought to civilization its own splendid offerings.

12. GO FORTH IN GOOD CHEER

"On you and on your generation will rest the task of righting this frightful wrong, of arresting this stupid waste.

". . . when your day comes go forth in good cheer. As a pioneer you will encounter stupidity and mental rubbish blocking and entangling your path. But, push on! For he who has both knowledge and understanding is not only doubly strong in his own day and generation, but will animate posterity."

LOUIS SULLIVAN

AND now it's up to you. The designers of contemporary houses and furniture can't do it all. They supply the professional leadership, but you must at least *consider* their suggestions. You must open your minds about your houses. You have always been adaptable to changing conditions, and in most cases you are quick to adopt improvements. For instance, with complete willingness —even eagerness—you have allowed contemporary designers to perfect your bathrooms and kitchens, but you have not shown anything like this progressive spirit about the rest of the house.

What do you really *know* about contemporary houses? You may have glanced at a few photographs in the magazines, or caught a glimpse of one or two as you drove past in your car. Perhaps the few examples you have seen have not appealed to you, but is this enough to cause you to close your mind to the whole idea?

Why not give them a chance? Study them—study their appearance, their plan, and the ideal that is behind them. Consciously pick out the ideas that appeal to you. And don't stop with one house. Steep yourself in this whole new concept of living. Study photographs, plans, materials, and the philosophy of the new architecture.* Subscribe to such magazines as *The Architectural Forum, Pencil Points, The Architectural Record,*

---

* See end of this book for suggested library.

and the California magazine *Arts & Architecture,* which make a point of publishing all that is new in the development of houses. If you give the new houses the opportunity to impress themselves on your consciousness as strongly as old houses have during the years of your life, I'll wager that when you build your house after the war, it will be a contemporary house.

Suppose you never come to the point of building your post-war dream house, wherever you live—a one-room apartment, a six-room cottage, or a twenty-five-room house—the way you furnish your interiors will reflect the knowledge you have received through your study of contemporary architecture. Who doesn't want spaciousness, light, air, cleanliness, and freedom in his surroundings? Contemporary architectural thinking will point the way for you.

It will teach you to overcome the fear of empty spaces. All the meaningless prints, ornamental mirrors, whatnots, crystal candelabra and wall brackets used to fill empty spaces will go. Ornamental draperies, valances and fancy tie-backs will disappear. No more oriental rugs, homesick for mosques and bazaars, where their harsh-colored elaboration belongs. You won't even miss them when your eye becomes familiar with floors covered in one unbroken restful color running from room to room throughout the house.

Your new furniture will be in a wood, the color and grain of which are left in their natural state. These new light-colored woods keep their clear colors indefinitely, and the transparent lacquers that preserve them require the minimum of labor, and none of the tedious attention enforced by older furniture. You will get a new pleasure from such woods, in contrast to the dark, stained, gloomy finishes of antique furniture. In contemporary furniture, the surfaces will be plain with none of the elaborately carved leaves, masks, and rocaille gathering the dust into every crevice, and requiring constant waxing and polishing to take away some of the dead ponderousness that keeps settling over it.

People are gradually losing their taste for massive furniture and masses of it. Rooms are no longer designed in the scale and particularly the height of the eighteenth-century rooms for which antique furniture was made, with the result that it appears awkward, bulky, and uncomfortable in our rooms today. Contemporary furniture will be scaled to the correct proportion for the new rooms. Hence it will be unobtrusive and quiet. There will be no feeling that you are in a museum and have been allowed to sit down in one of the period rooms.

And comfort—everyone really wants to be comfortable. Every chair and sofa should feel good to sit in, and this is easily arranged in contemporary interiors, where no concessions have to be made to period chairs and loveseats to keep up the pseudo-old-world atmosphere, and to make a pretty historical picture.

Chairs are now being designed to fit the body, an idea never really attempted before. This, you must agree, is an improvement over antique chairs, particularly antique dining chairs, which invariably are of such back-breaking discomfort that a prolonged meal can become an agonizing endurance test for certain parts of the anatomy.

Dining tables are beginning to take on a new adaptability under the guidance of contemporary designers. They are flexible, expanding to accommodate a dozen people and shrinking to suit two; and doing this easily by means of folding sections or demountable ends, so that it is no longer necessary to assemble the entire household in order to adjust them.

Contemporary rooms are equally beautiful by day or night, which cannot be said for the older type of room. These older rooms with dark walls, dark furniture, heavy draperies, and dark paintings are gloomy and stuffy in contrast to the sunlight outside the windows—a feeling that only disappears when it is night, and the artificial light makes the rooms more cheerful by contrast. Contemporary rooms are lighter in tone, with the walls and upholstery in bright clear colors. The windows are bigger and not smothered to death with hangings; in fact, very often they have nothing but venetian blinds to control the sunlight which pours into the room, sweeping out the shadows, and blending with the colors inside as naturally as with the landscape outside.

Contemporary houses are the natural development of architecture to meet the changing forms in our social habits and customs. The forbidding formality in the social behavior of earlier periods was expressed by an equally forbidding formality in the houses and furniture with which these people lived. The active outdoor life and the informality of living and entertaining today require a whole new concept of houses and furniture. Contemporary planning is the answer.

The new houses and their interiors are the new way of life of a new generation. They show a complete consciousness of today. They do not look to the past in envy nor to the future in wishful anticipation. They have come to perfect terms with the present. Wouldn't you enjoy the feeling that you are at one with the contemporary life that is the expression of this generation; that your house is tuned in to this moment in time; that you are glad to be living in the twentieth century—rather proud, in fact, to be a part of it?

SUGGESTED READING

SUGGESTED LIBRARY FOR READERS INTERESTED IN CONTEMPORARY DESIGN

FORD, JAMES and KATHERINE MORROW: *Design of Modern Interiors*. New York: Architectural Book Publishing Co. Inc.; 1942.

FORD, JAMES and KATHERINE MORROW: *The Modern House in America*. New York: Architectural Book Publishing Co. Inc.; 1940.

GIEDION-WELCKER, C.: *Modern Plastic Art*. Zürich: Dr. H. Gireberger; 1937.

GIEDION, SIGFRIED: *Space, Time and Architecture*. Cambridge: The Harvard University Press; 1941.

GUTHEIM, FREDERICK, editor: *Frank Lloyd Wright on Architecture*. New York: Duell, Sloan and Pearce; 1941

HAMLIN, TALBOT: *Architecture Through the Ages*. New York: G. P. Putnam's Sons; 1940.

HITCHCOCK, HENRY-RUSSELL: *In the Nature of Materials*. New York: Duell, Sloan and Pearce; 1942.

MARTIN, J. L., NICHOLSON, BEN, GABO, N., editors: *Circle*. London: Faber and Faber Limited; 1937.

MORRISON, HUGH: *Louis Sullivan*. New York: W. W. Norton & Company, Inc.: 1935.

RAYMOND, ANTONIN: *Architectural Details*. New York: The Architectural Forum; 1938.

READ, HERBERT: *Art and Industry*. New York: Harcourt, Brace and Company; 1938.

ROTH, ALFRED: *The New Architecture*. Zürich: Dr. H. Girsberger; 1940.

SERT, JOSE LUIS: *Can Our Cities Survive?* Cambridge: The Harvard University Press; 1942.

The author suggests that those readers beginning their study of contemporary houses should start with the two books on the above list by James Ford and Katherine Morrow Ford.

A NOTE ON THE TYPE

The text of this book is set on the Linotype in Fairfield, the first type-face from the hand of the distinguished American artist and engraver Rudolph Ruzicka. In its structure Fairfield displays the sober and sane qualities of a master craftsman whose talent has long been dedicated to clarity. It is this trait that accounts for the trim grace and virility, the spirited design and sensitive balance of this original type face.

COMPOSED, PRINTED, AND BOUND BY
H. WOLFF, NEW YORK

TYPOGRAPHY AND BINDING DESIGN BY
STEFAN SALTER